MENDELSSOHN IN SCOTLAND

Mendelssohn in Scotland

DAVID JENKINS & MARK VISOCCHI

CHAPPELL & COMPANY
in association with
ELM TREE BOOKS

Chappell & Company Limited
50 New Bond Street, London W1A 2BR

LONDON AMSTERDAM BRUSSELS HAMBURG
JOHANNESBURG MADRID MILAN PARIS
STOCKHOLM SYDNEY TORONTO WELLINGTON
ZURICH NEW YORK

First Published 1978
© David Jenkins & Mark Visocchi, 1978

Designed by Peter Ducker

Typeset by Western Printing Services Ltd, Avonmouth, Bristol
Printed in Great Britain by
Fletcher & Son Ltd, Norwich

Production in association with
Book Production Consultants, Cambridge

ISBN 0 903443 18 X

To Fiona

Contents

List of Illustrations

9

The First Twenty Years

Berlin: March 26, 1829

NEXT AUGUST I AM GOING TO SCOTLAND, with a rake for folksongs, an ear for the lovely, fragrant countryside, and a heart for the the bare legs of the natives.

Klingemann, you must join me, we may lead a royal life! Demolish obstacles and fly to Scotland.

[FMB]

Felix Mendelssohn-Bartholdy left Berlin on April 10, 1829 with his father and sister, Rebecka, who accompanied him as far as Hamburg. Mendelssohn was not a good sailor and found the North Sea crossing to England extremely unpleasant, but on arrival in London his spirits soon revived when, in the company of Carl Klingemann and friends, he was caught up in a round of social and musical activities. Four days after his arrival in London he wrote to his family:

London is the grandest and most complicated monster on the face of the earth. How can I compress into one letter what I have been three days seeing? I hardly remember the chief events and yet I must not keep a diary, for then I should see less of life, and that must not be. On the contrary, I want to catch hold of whatever offers itself to me. Things roll and whirl round me and carry me along in a vortex.

Such was the close relationship between Mendelssohn and members of his family, a relationship perhaps born of a need to sustain the bonds of a family whose religion set it apart from the bulk of the German community, that it was natural for him to tell them of his impressions of the English capital at the earliest opportunity.

The story of the Mendelssohn family begins in 1743 with the arrival in Berlin of a ragged Jewish boy, Moses Mendelssohn, the son of a poor Jewish schoolmaster from Dessau on the Elbe. In 1762 Moses married Fromet Gugenheim, the daughter of a wealthy Hamburg family. Through a combination of hard work and some talent Moses built up for himself a considerable reputation as a philosopher and a modest income. His acceptance

J. W. Childe's watercolour portrait of Mendelssohn (1829)

Moses Mendelssohn (1729–1786), grandfather of Felix
Note the layout of the spelling of the Mendelssohn name on this portrait of Moses.
The name Mendelssohn implies the relationship 'son of Mendel' in Jewish Germany (as
Donaldson implies the relationship 'son of Donald' in Britain), and in so doing follows the
normal Jewish way of forming a name.

as a philosophical writer (*Phädon* – a dialogue upon the immortality of the
soul, based on Plato's *Phaedo*, was published in Berlin in 1767) was greatly
helped by the growing spirit of toleration encouraged by the leading writers
and thinkers of the eighteenth-century Enlightenment. Their efforts helped
to mitigate the virulent anti-Jewish attitudes which had previously forced
Jews to seek security through settling in communities of their own kind.

Abraham Mendelssohn (1776–1835), father of Felix

> *Despise my people if you will.*
> *Neither I nor you have chosen our people. Are we*
> *Our people? People? What means then the people?*
> *Are Jew and Christian rather Jew and Christian?*
> *Than men?*

These lines from a speech by the main character, Nathan, a Jew, in Lessing's play *Nathan the Wise* (1779) express the attitude of a prominent thinker of the Enlightenment to religious toleration. If the sense of these words is allusive, the career of Moses Mendelssohn was nevertheless assisted by the growth of such ideas, and it is interesting to note that Lessing and

Lea Mendelssohn, née Salomon (1777–1842), mother of Felix

Mendelssohn were, in fact, close friends; the character of Nathan was
consciously modelled on that of Mendelssohn.

Called Abraham after his grandfather Gugenheim, the second son of
Moses and Fromet went to Paris and became cashier in Fould's bank there
in 1803, but in 1804 he resigned his post and went into partnership with his
elder brother Joseph. In December of the same year Abraham Mendelssohn
married Lea Salomon, of a Jewish family from Berlin, and settled in Hamburg
in a house in the Grosse Michaelisstrasse. Abraham's business, which he
carried on from this house, seems to have been doing sufficiently well
financially at this time for the family to afford a house out of town, and it
was called 'Marten's Mühle'.

Hamburg port in the eighteenth century

Politically Hamburg was a much freer city than Berlin, and in the days before the unification of Germany Hamburg itself was one of the vast number of independent states. Commercially, it formed the headquarters of the Hanseatic traders and was well placed as a location for the banking house which Abraham and Joseph established at the fortuitous time when expanding commerce needed the credit facilities which such a house could provide. The rise of the Mendelssohn family from abject poverty to considerable fortune within two generations illuminates the way in which it was possible to accomplish this transformation in the changing world of the eighteenth century.

In the early years of the nineteenth century, Napoleon, then effective ruler of most of Europe as of France, tried to starve Britain into submission by closing all continental ports to trade. He declared:

> *England will find her vessels laden with useless wealth wandering round the high seas, where they claim to rule as sole masters, seeking in vain from the Sound to the Hellespont for a port to open and receive them.*

Far from winning over the hearts and minds of the peoples of Europe

Fanny Cäcilie, Felix Mendelssohn's elder sister

his conquests fostered a sense of national identity as a means of resisting
French aggressiveness. Before moving to Hamburg Abraham had lived
happily in Paris, but under the pressure of French military intervention
he gradually identified himself as an upholder of German nationalism; this
implied both a resistance to French domination and a support for the idea of
a federation of all the Germanic states. Three children were born to him and
Lea in Hamburg: Fanny Cäcilie (November, 1805), Jacob Ludwig Felix
(February, 1809) and Rebecka (April, 1811). Eventually, as Napoleon
tightened his grip on the continental ports, Abraham was forced to leave
Hamburg, taking his children and his now considerable wealth with him.
On reaching Berlin Abraham contributed some of his wealth to the cause of
the Prussian military effort against Napoleon and his generosity was

Rebecka, his younger sister

rewarded by election to the Berlin municipal council – a striking contrast to his father's original reception in the Prussian capital.

Napoleon's conquests in Europe had other than physical implications: as promoter of the ideas lying behind the French Revolution he actually helped the cause of the Jews by urging 'Liberty, Equality, Fraternity' for all the people of the countries he dominated, and the year 1812 saw Napoleon decree in principle the legal emancipation of German Jews. The French Revolution of 1789 demonstrated the ephemeral nature of any political and social structure, and the wars which followed the French Revolution tumbled many of the ancient families of Europe.

In Berlin, eleven days after Napoleon's defeat at the batttle of Leipzig following Austria's declaration of war against Napoleon, Abraham's second son and youngest child, Paul, was born (October, 1813).

The tolerant attitudes of the Enlightenment which contributed to the emancipation of the Jews were also characterised by a distrust of religious practices and greatly influenced Moses's religious breadth of view. It was

Paul, his younger brother

possibly under his influence that his family adopted that same lack of any really deep religious convictions which resulted in a break with the Jewish faith. The daughters of Moses Mendelssohn, Dorothea and Henriette, became Roman Catholics. The sons remained Jews, but eventually Abraham saw that the change was inevitable, and decided to have his children baptised and brought up as Protestant Christians. It was on the advice and example of Lea's brother, Salomon Bartholdy, that the conversion was finally decided, and to whom the adoption of the name Bartholdy was due, it being the name of the former proprietor of the garden belonging to the Salomon family! Abraham Mendelssohn perhaps shared the feelings towards conversion of the German Jewish poet, Heinrich Heine, who looked on his own baptism as a ticket of admission into European culture. Six years after the baptism of his

19

son, Felix, Abraham did in fact become a Christian, but it is doubtful whether for him this action was more than a mere formality.

Abraham Mendelssohn described his position in life by saying 'Formerly I was the son of my father, now I am the father of my son.' He also looked on himself as a mere 'dash' (–) between father and son. No doubt somewhat overshadowed by Moses, the philosopher, and Felix, the musician, he nevertheless underestimated his qualities of judgement and perception not only on lifemanship but also on artistic matters. Felix respected his insight into music despite the fact that his father was not a technical musician, and always paid deference to the judgement of his father.

> *I am often quite unable to understand how it is possible to have so accurate a judgement about music without being a technical musician, and if I could only say what I feel in the same clear and intelligent manner that you always do, I would certainly never make another confused speech as long as I live.*
> [FMB: March, 1835]

Felix Mendelssohn-Bartholdy was three years old when the family escaped to Berlin. His mother was a highly educated woman, a polyglot, a good pianist, and read Homer in the original. Felix and his sister Fanny had every encouragement to develop their abilities. Musical education began with five-minute piano lessons from mother, and Felix's progress was not rushed; before long it was he who set the learning pace, leaving his mother and sister to wonder at his precocity. Other aspects of a general education were not neglected; Mendelssohn was taught dancing and gymnastics, and this early training in physical activities provided two pastimes he enjoyed throughout his life.

On a visit to Paris by Joseph and Abraham Mendelssohn in 1816 for the liquidation of the indemnity to be paid by France to Prussia on account of the war, Abraham took his family with him, and Fanny and Felix, then aged eleven and seven respectively, had piano lessons from Madame Bigot. Soon after their return from Paris to the grandmother's house at the Neue Promenade in Berlin, where the family still lived, the children's education seems to have started in earnest. Literary subjects were taught by K. W. L. Heyse (father of Paul Heyse, the novelist), piano by Ludwig Berger of the Clementi/John Field school, violin by Henning, a member of the opera orchestra, and harmony, counterpoint and composition by Karl Friedrich Zelter. Felix had Rösel as a tutor for landscape drawing.

Aged nine, Mendelssohn made his first appearance in public at a concert given on October 28, 1818; he played the piano part of a trio for pianoforte and two horns, and was much applauded.

The Mendelssohn children were worked hard at their lessons, and Felix said in later years how much they enjoyed their Sundays, because they were not forced to get up at five o'clock in the morning to work!

Aged eleven, he entered the singing class of the *Singakademie* as an alto. Devrient tells how he took his place for the Friday practices

> *amongst the grown-up people in his child's dress, a tight-fitting jacket, cut very low at the neck, over which the wide trousers were buttoned; into the slanting pockets of these the little fellow liked to thrust his hands, rocking his curly head from side to side, and shifting restlessly from one foot to the other.*

Aged twelve, Felix began to compose systematically, and from 1820 dates the first of forty-four volumes in which Mendelssohn methodically preserved to the time of his death autographed copies of his published and unpublished compositions.

One morning in the spring of 1821 Weber was walking through the streets of Berlin with his pupil Jules Benedict when a boy ran up and introduced himself as Felix Mendelssohn-Bartholdy. Weber was due at a rehearsal, but Benedict was dragged off to the Mendelssohn home and made to play excerpts from Weber's newly-completed *Der Freischütz* [*The Huntsmen*]. In return for this favour the boy played from memory a number of Bach fugues and Cramer studies. Calling again at the house a few days later Benedict caught Felix at work on what was to become his Opus 1.

> *I found him on a footstool, before a small table, writing with great earnestness some music. On my asking what he was about, he replied, gravely, 'I am finishing my new Quartet for piano and stringed instruments'.*
>
> *I could not resist my boyish curiosity to examine this composition, and, looking over his shoulder, saw as beautiful a score as if it had been written by the most skilful copyist. It was his first Quartet in C minor.*
>
> *Then forgetting quartets and Weber, down we went into the garden, he clearing high hedges with a leap, running, singing, and climbing up the trees like a squirrel – the very image of health and happiness.*

During the period that Abraham worked in Paris, he called on Goethe at Frankfurt and was instrumental in bringing together Goethe and Zelter, who had set some of the poet's songs. Zelter had Felix as a pupil, and it was

Johann Wolfgang von Goethe (1749–1832)

through his friendship with Goethe that in due course Felix was taken to see Goethe at Weimar. The boy's enthusiasm for meeting the old German poet can be gauged from a letter written to his parents describing the visit.

> *Professor Zelter came and said: 'Goethe is here – the old gentleman is here'! and at once we were down the steps and in Goethe's house. He was in the garden and just coming round a hedge. Isn't it strange, dear father? That*

was exactly how you met him. He is very friendly, but I find all his pictures unlike him. Then he looked at his interesting collection of fossils which his son had arranged for him and kept saying: 'H'm, h'm! I am very much pleased'. After that I walked in the garden with him and Professor Zelter for half an hour. Then came dinner. One would never take him for seventy-three, but for fifty. After dinner Fraulein Ulrike, the sister of Frau von Goethe [the wife of Goethe's son], asked for a kiss and I did the same. Every morning I get a kiss from the author of Faust *and* Werther *and every afternoon two kisses from Father and Friend Goethe. Think of that!!*
[FMB: November 6, 1821]

In the summer of 1822 the Mendelssohn family undertook a tour in Switzerland. Starting on July 6, they travelled to Cassel, Frankfurt, Darmstadt Schaffhausen, Amsteg, Interlaken, Vevey and Chamonix. The trip, made in a large and merry family party of ten, introduced Felix to the joys of travel, and his compositions reveal a readiness to assimilate external ideas, a quality which proved to be of great importance in Felix's later development as a composer.

An important event in the summer of 1824 was a visit by Abraham, Felix and Rebecka to Dobberan, a bathing place on the shores of the Baltic near Rostock. For the wind-band at Dobberan spa Felix wrote an overture, but the most important result of the visit was that Felix there, for the first time, saw the sea. Unlike the Swiss journey, the period of absorbing his impressions and incorporating them into his music was longer, and it was four years later before the *Meeresstille* [*Calm Sea*] overture translated these impressions into sound.

Among the great performers whom Felix met at this time was Moscheles. En route from Vienna to Paris and London he stayed in Berlin for six weeks in November and December 1824, and called almost daily at the Mendelssohns'. After a time, at the request of Felix's parents, he was prevailed upon to give their son regular piano lessons every other day. Himself only thirty years old, Moscheles was reluctant to give the lessons, being only too well aware of Felix's great gifts. He wrote of the Mendelssohns' home and children:

a family such as I have never known before; Felix a mature artist, and yet but fifteen; Fanny extraordinarily gifted, playing Bach's fugues by heart and with astonishing correctness – in fact, a thorough musician. The parents gave me the impression of people of the highest cultivation. They are very

23

far from being over-fond of their children; indeed, they are in anxiety about Felix's future, whether his gifts are lasting, and will lead to a solid, permanent future, or whether he may not suddenly collapse, like so many other gifted children.

He has no need of lessons; if he wishes to take a hint from me as to anything new to him, he can easily do so.

In 1825 Abraham Mendelssohn undertook a journey to Paris to fetch his sister Henriette back to Germany. Felix went with him, and he plunged at once into Parisian musical society. Hummel, Kreutzer, Meyerbeer, Rossini, and many more were glad to meet the wonderful boy, but the French musicians made a bad impression on Mendelssohn; it was mainly their ignorance of German music, including such masterpieces as Beethoven's *Fidelio*, and the general cultivation amongst the French musicians of virtuosity as an end in itself which Mendelssohn disliked.

The Mendelssohns were beginning to outgrow the accommodation of the house at 7 Neue Promenade, and at the end of the summer of 1825 they moved to a large house situated in grounds at 3 Leipziger Strasse. Originally situated in a quiet suburb of Berlin, nothing now remains of the main house with its many rooms, or the several guest houses and spacious park with its lime trees, rose bushes, yew alley and fountain, where the boy loved the freedom to ride his horse. On Sundays the large rooms of the main house were given over to musicales which starred the young Felix. Moscheles has preserved programmes for two of the Sunday concerts which took place before the Mendelssohns moved to Leipziger Strasse and these can be regarded as typical of such meetings:

November 28, 1824
Morning music at the Mendelssohns':
  Felix's C minor Quartet
  Felix's D major Symphony
  Concerto by Bach played by Fanny
  Duet for Two Pianos in D minor by Samuel Arnold [Organist at
    Westminster Abbey in London circa 1800]

December 12, 1824
Sunday music at the Mendelssohns':
  Felix's F minor Quartet
  Duet in G for Two Pianos played by Moscheles [and Mendelssohn?]
  Hummel's Trio in G played by little Schilling

The Mendelssohns' house and garden in Berlin

His early compositions are dominated by the overture to *A Midsummer Night's Dream* which Mendelssohn composed during the fine summer of 1826 in the charming surroundings of the new garden of 3 Leipziger Strasse. Composed as a result of Mendelssohn's contact with Shakespeare's plays, the overture was first performed as a duet on the piano, and later by an orchestra in the Mendelssohns' garden-house. With its composition his musical apprenticeship could be said to have finished, and his lessons with Zelter were discontinued.

On May 2, 1826 he had entered the University of Berlin where his tutor was Heyse, now a professor. It is not known whether Felix went through the normal university course or not, but he certainly attended Hegel's lectures on aesthetics; he left an impression on Mendelssohn's receptive mind which perhaps goes some way to explain the composer's tendency to organise his Romantic musical ideas within classical frameworks. Hegel's views were that:

> *Like any other art music must retain the emotions and their manifestations lest the music plunge into bacchanalian clamour and whirl into a tumult of passion. . . Music must remain untrammelled and yet in its outpouring serene. . . The proper domain of music is essentially that of inwardness combined with tone unalloyed. . . In music, objectivity abates. Being the essentially Romantic art, music withdraws altogether into subjectivity, both as regards inner meaning and outer manifestation.*

Felix took special pleasure in the lectures of Carl Ritter in geography, and he continued work on landscape drawing which he had already worked at for several years; both these studies were to be potentially useful to him in his travels abroad.

The change to the new house was a great event in the family life, and the garden was an attraction to the friends of the Mendelssohn household. In addition to the well-established intellectuals such as Hegel, Heine and Droysen, young people flocked to the house more than ever. One of the features of garden life was a domestic newspaper which in summer was called *The Garden Times* and in winter *Tea and Snow Times*. This paper appears to have been edited by Felix, but anyone was free to contribute, and pens, ink and paper lay in one of the summer-houses for this purpose. Mendelssohn was the centre of attraction in this social milieu, but it was soon to lose one of its cleverest and most genial members, for late in 1827 Carl Klingemann left the set to go to London as Secretary to the Hanoverian Legation. Fanny Mendelssohn echoed the feelings of her family in a letter to Klingemann written shortly after his departure for London:

In conclusion, I must tell you that we miss you and long for you very much. Ah, Mr. Klingemann, who is there now to criticise our embroideries, our new dresses, or our bonnets? Who drops in en passant for half an hour's chat? Who understands nonsense, and knows how other honest people feel? All these inestimable qualities, as well as the praiseworthy dexterity with which you handle the German language, must now perish in London.

If the year 1827 saw the departure of a good friend from the Mendelssohn circle, it also saw the fruition of an encounter of a different sort: Mendelssohn's lifelong love affair with the music of J. S. Bach. The young Mendelssohn declared of one Bach chorus that, 'If life had taken faith and hope from me, this single chorus would restore all.' But Mendelssohn was not alone in his enthusiasm for Bach; Goethe praised Bach for his music's mystical qualities, and Hegel spoke of him as 'The master, whose grand, truly Protestant, pithy yet learned genius we have only lately come to value again properly.' Karl Zelter admired Bach greatly, and from time to time performed some of the shorter Bach works at his concerts in the *Singakademie*. He had a copy of the *St Matthew Passion*, but believed that musically the work was too complex for contemporary audiences. In 1824 Felix was given as a Christmas present from his grandmother a copy of the *St Matthew Passion* which she possibly transcribed herself from Zelter's copy. Mendelssohn began rehearsing the work with a small choir in his own home in 1827, and in 1829 he succeeded in gaining Zelter's permission for a public performance at the *Singakademie*. March 11, which was set as the date of the performance, was the centenary of both the original performance of the work and the birth of Moses Mendelssohn. The first performance was a sell-out, and Zelter commented enthusiastically on the success of this performance to Goethe. Because there were approaching one thousand disappointed applicants for tickets, the work was given a second performance attended by Hegel, and a third performance was directed by Zelter himself, after Mendelssohn had left for London.

The Grandest and most Complicated Monster
on the Face of the Earth

There can be little doubt that Klingemann's letters from London to the Mendelssohn household built up Felix's expectations as regards the musical and social activities of the capital:

When under the influence of the thick air the body commands the intellect; when one is obliged to take large quantities of classical mutton, half-cooked vegetables, praiseworthy apple pie, and heavy port wine as a counter weight to the ponderous air; when, again, valiantly walking the immense distances of the city, one must swallow the heavy air in behalf of the heavy fare, and then sleep an endless time to be able to walk again, and by means of the walking be able to eat again, and so on.

'How do you like England?' is the question with which every miss or mistress to whom I get introduced assails me, and being by this time prepared for it I invariably parry the thrust by boldly answering, 'Exceeding well!' And that is perfect truth, for everything here is so attractively different from what we foreigners are accustomed (mixed at the same time with such unexpected politeness to a stranger) that I believe it may sufficiently occupy one's intent for years.

This English comfort is the laziest fellow I ever met with. He gets up at ten o'clock, then he enters his cosy little room, about half as lofty as the one in the Berlin embassy, but nicely furnished; a cheerful coal fire is blazing in the chimney, the water is boiling, the breakfast table ready, and everything upon it placed in proper symmetry – but with a special relish the eye rests upon an immeasurable newspaper, with leading articles, news, lawsuits, police reports, and various scandal.

We 'do' Spohr, myself drumming the bass in the overture at four hands with a young lady, then all of us encircling the piano in a row like organ pipes and singing –

Cold and stiff and yet majestic,
On the shutter there he lies.

We also play trios by Hummel and Beethoven, but I do not play the violin; then some of Beethoven's symphonies at four hands, and whist at eight hands.
When, shortly after my arrival, I was a little hoarse, they asked me,

'Haben Sie auch schön einen Kalten gefangen?' I translated it into English, 'Have you caught a cold already?' and then I understood it.

I only wish I were less near-sighted, especially for the sake of the English ladies. They do not know how to bake a pancake, and are mostly occupied with useless things, but they look desperately pretty.

I never see these stages [coaches] without pleasure. The big carriage, on which the passengers cling like wasps on a sweet pear, rolls so swiftly and merrily along that my heart rejoices at the thought of next spring, when the stage, with its team of four strong horses, is to convey me eighty miles a day along the smooth roads and across the green, hilly country, full of towns, villages, and cottages, to Scotland.

But London is too large: I told them so at once. They do not, however, listen to me, and go on building at quite a ridiculous rate. The houses will at last be obliged to hire the people, instead of the reverse: there's no end to be seen of it, and the monster may yet swallow many a village before it is satisfied.

But the city is the best of all, and to struggle on through the quantity of carriages, coal-heavers, rogues, and honest people to where, in the neighbourhood of the Bank, Birch's famous mock-turtle soup is to be had, affords real pleasure.

And everything is so long here! I believe Beethoven must have been an Englishman. The oysters, however, are elegantly small.

[CK, London: December 7, 1827]

For Klingemann, however, England was not without its drawbacks: the gloom of the British Sunday and the difficulty of pronouncing the English 'th'. While finding features of English life strange, Klingemann himself, with his serious expression and ministerial manners, was a source of good-natured amusement to his friends among the young ladies of London society. Carl Klingemann was eleven years older than Mendelssohn, and as the son of a poet and theatre director he was accustomed to the arts, and was himself something of a poet. In London his house frequently served as a home for Felix, and being highly regarded in British court circles his friendship gave Mendelssohn easy access to the upper social echelons. As an indication of the special relationship between Felix and Klingemann, the year before he died Felix called him 'My one and only friend.'

The *Attwood*, with Mendelssohn aboard, sailed from Hamburg on Saturday, April 18, and did not reach London until noon on Tuesday, April 21. As can be judged from the duration of the crossing, the passage was a very bad one;

30

Carl Klingemann

the engines broke down, and Mendelssohn lay prostrate with seasickness for
the whole of Sunday and Monday.

> *From Saturday evening to Monday afternoon we had contrary winds, and*
> *such a storm that all on board were ill. We had once to stop for a while*
> *on account of a dense fog, and then again in order to repair the engine; even*
> *last night at the mouth of the Thames we were obliged to cast anchor to*
> *avoid a collision with other ships. Fancy, moreover, that from Sunday*
> *morning to Monday evening I had one fainting fit after another, from*
> *disgust with myself and everything about the boat, cursing England, and*
> *particularly my own* Meeresstille, *and scolding the waiter with all my might.*
> [FMB, London: April 21, 1829]

31

His visit to England was the first stage of a long European journey planned with care by his father and lasting for the next three years of his life. On this journey he was

> *closely to examine the various countries, and to fix on one in which to live and work; to make his name and abilities known so that where he settled he should not be received as a stranger; and lastly to employ his good fortune in life, and the liberality of his father, in preparing the ground for future efforts.*
> [FMB: February, 1832]

Mendelssohn was welcomed on landing by Carl Klingemann, and went to stay at a house which was then numbered 103 Portland Street. It was the middle of the musical season, and on the night of his arrival in London the great singer, Malibran, made an appearance at the opera as Desdemona. To judge from his letter of April 25 her performance obviously impressed Mendelssohn greatly.

> *I got a seat in the pit (half a guinea) – a large house,* [Italian opera, King's Theatre] *decorated with crimson, six tiers of boxes with crimson curtains, out of which peep the ladies, bedecked with great white feathers, chains, jewels of all kinds. An odour of pomade and perfume assails you as you enter, which gave me a headache: in the pit all the gentlemen, with fresh-trimmed whiskers, the house crowded, the orchestra very good, conducted by a Signor Spagnoletti (in December I will give you an imitation of him which will make you die of laughter). Donzelli (Othello), a bravura performer ingeniously ornamental, shouts and forces his voice tremendously, almost constantly sings a little to high, but with no end of* haut goût *(for instance, in the last passionate scene, where Malibran screams and raves almost disagreeably, instead of shouting the recitatives, as he usually does, he drops his voice, so that the last bars are scarcely audible). Mme. Malibran is a young woman, beautiful and splendidly made, her hair* en troupet, *full of fire and power, very coquettish, setting off her performance partly with very clever embellishments of her own invention, partly with imitations from Pasta (it impressed me strangely to see her take the harp and sing the whole scene exactly like Pasta, and copy her also in that vaguely floating passage which I am sure you, dear father, must remember). She plays beautifully, her attitudes are good, and it is only a pity she should so often exaggerate and then nearly touch the ridiculous and disagreeable.*
> [FMB, London: April 25, 1829]

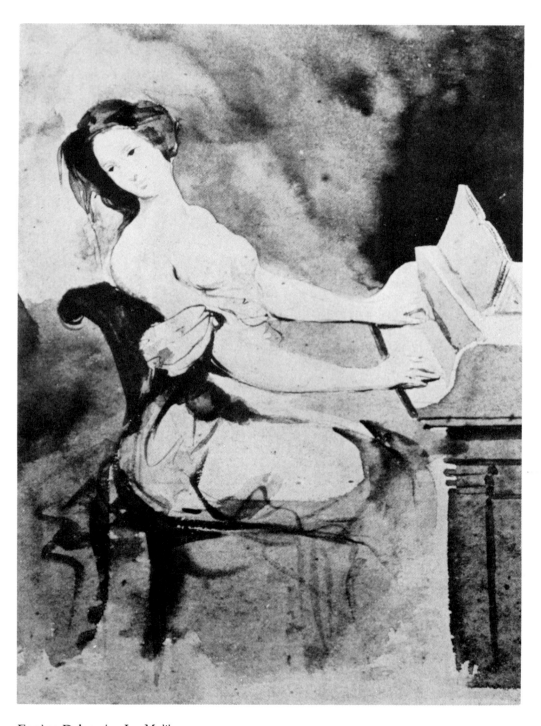

Eugène Delacroix: *La Malibran*

33

His first appearance before an English audience was at the Philharmonic concert in the Argyll Rooms on May 25 when he conducted his Symphony in C minor. Mendelssohn was deeply touched by the warmth of his reception, and published the symphony with a dedication to the Philharmonic. They replied by electing him an honorary member of the Society on November 29. His concerts brought him before the musical public of London, but they did not do much to provide him with a living since the only commission he received, and was forced for obvious reasons to decline, was for a festival hymn for Ceylon to celebrate the emancipation of the natives. The idea of the commission appealed to his sense of humour, and he signed a letter dated June 9: 'Composer to the Island of Ceylon'.

Mendelssohn found time for activities other than music: he visited the House of Commons, picture galleries, balls at Devonshire House and Landsdowne House, and so many other parties that his family in Berlin thought he was giving up music for a life of pleasure, and indeed their worries were possibly well-founded to judge from an amusing little anecdote about Mendelssohn and his friends, Rosen and Mühlenfeld, coming home late from a state dinner given by the Prussian ambassador. On the way they bought three German sausages, found a quiet street in which to eat them, and regaled the neighbourhood with a three-part song and peals of laughter between the mouthfuls. He also found time to have his portrait painted by James Warren Childe. This pictures him as handsome, slim, confident and perhaps looking something of a dandy.

FELIX
MENDELSSOHN
BARTHOLDY.

Aubrey Beardsley's portrait of Mendelssohn, from *The Savoy* magazine 1896

35

To York and Edinburgh

Late in July Mendelssohn and Klingemann left London for Edinburgh, stopping off at York on July 23 and Durham on July 24. The progress of their journey can be traced by Felix's sketches.

The first part of their journey north from London to Stamford would have taken Mendelssohn and Klingemann something like twenty hours by coach. The period 1830–1850 was the heyday of coach travel, and the fact that the

Mendelssohn: sketch of York (July 23, 1829)

37

same journey would have taken two days in 1706, according to a bill advertising the York Four Days Stage-Coach, is a measure of the advances which had taken place over the previous hundred years. No longer was it necessary to rest up for a whole night en route before setting off again on the rutted tracks of the North Road first thing in the morning; Mendelssohn would have stopped off for only three or four minutes at staging posts while the horses were changed.

The first stage coach ran between Chester and York in 1567 and was the result of a transformation of the typical waggon which was used for the transport of goods from 1500 on roads often knee-deep in mud. The original coaches had a wooden body covered in leather, no windows or doors, and heavy curtains were the only protection against the weather, but it was not long before the installation of windows and doors became common. Compared with travel on horseback at an average five miles-per-hour these early coaches were much slower, and the traveller was fortunate to average a speed of two miles-per-hour even using teams of eight horses. Queen Elizabeth I preferred speedier travel on horseback and complained that coaching caused her too much discomfort to be tolerated. About 1750 one significant development took place in the coaching system: waggons and coaches changed horses at predetermined points along their routes, and with the gradual flowering of trade in the provinces the new stage coach system could offer much-improved communication with the capital. A combination of coach design improvements, better roads and shorter stages of approximately ten miles between horse changes meant that coaches were able to keep up an average speed far beyond what had previously been possible.

In 1829 five thousand coaches covered twelve thousand miles of British roads every night, and thirty thousand men and one hundred and fifty thousand horses were required to service the system. Mendelssohn and Klingemann had the option of using mail coach or stage coach on their journey from London to Edinburgh. The mail coaches were painted red, maroon and black with the royal arms featured on the door panels. The stage coaches on the other hand were much less restrained in their decoration, and the fierce competition for business on the routes from London was reflected in bright coach colourings to attract the customer and the adoption of names such as Red Rover and Tally-Ho which made advertising a specific coach easy.

The usual departure place from London for mail coaches before 1829 was the General Post Office in Lombard Street, but Mendelssohn was possibly amongst the first travellers to leave from the new Post Office building at St Martins-le-Grand from where the mail coaches departed each morning at

Mendelssohn: Durham Cathedral from the west (July 24, 1829)
This formal pencil drawing on cartridge paper shows a fine sense of architectural
perspective and the precision of the Cathedral illustration is highlighted by its being viewed
through an arch of foliage.

eight o'clock, the northbound coaches making their way out of London via
Aldersgate Street.
 Klingemann's fascination with language would have been stirred by some
of the distinctive coaching expressions which stemmed from habits and ideas
peculiar to this form of transport, and which are still in common use: a
'backhander' was the tip given to the coach driver leaning down from his
seat at the front of the coach as the passenger disembarked; an 'outsider'

Coach outside the Bull & Mouth, St. Martins-le-Grand, by Shayer

was the name applied to a passenger occupying one of the cheaper seats on the outside of the coach which exposed the traveller to the rigour of the elements; 'dropping off' literally meant falling asleep and dropping off the coach!

One of the inns at which Mendelssohn and Klingemann's coach would have stopped on the Great North Road was the Bell Inn at Stilton, and in common with so many of the inns where coach parties stopped for refreshment it provided local delicacies to tempt the traveller. In the case of the Bell Inn it was widely known for its quality of cheese, but, in fact, the cheeses sold at the Bell Inn were not made in Stilton but many miles away in Leicestershire.

40

On the road north one of the major stopping places was the George Inn, Stamford, and while the horses were being changed Mendelssohn and Klingemann would have joined the passengers in the Down Waiting Room for York, while those heading for London sat in the Up Waiting Room – hence the phrase 'Going up to London'. The coming and going of passengers would have been almost continuous since forty or so coaches per day used the facilities of the George. By 1830 the cost of the journey as far as Stamford was £3.10s for the ten-hour trip, but it could be almost halved if one was prepared to travel outside. If the price of coach travel seems relatively high, one should remember that the coaching industry was labour-intensive, and the standard of service was good.

As a musician Mendelssohn would either have been fascinated or infuriated by the sound of the coaching horn blown by the guard. Though they may seem today to be a quaint relic, the coaching horn calls were in fact highly functional; traditional melodies were used as signature tunes by each coach so that the innkeeper would know which one was coming. A book of coaching horn calls gives in musical notation various tunes which had clearly defined meanings: 'The Start' meant that the coach was ready for departure; 'Clear the Road' was used to tell the toll-keeper to open the turnpike gates so that the mail was not held up (mail coaches passed free of toll charges); 'Change Horses', blown within a quarter mile of the inn, warned the ostlers to have the new team of horses ready to replace the tired animals.

The two travellers arrived in Edinburgh on July 26, 1829.

Impressions of the Scottish Capital

Edinburgh: July 28, 1829

It is Sunday when we arrive in Edinburgh; then we cross the meadows, going towards two desperately steep rocks, which are called Arthur's Seat, and climb up. Below on the green are walking the most variegated people, women, children, and cows; the city stretches far and wide; in the midst is the castle, like a bird's nest on a cliff; beyond the castle come meadows, then hills, then a broad river; beyond the river again hills; then a mountain rather more stern, on which towers Stirling Castle; then blue distance begins; further on you perceive a faint shadow, which they call Ben Lomond.

All this is but one half of Arthur's Seat; the other is simple enough,

Mendelssohn: Edinburgh skyline from Arthur's Seat

43

it is the great blue sea, immeasurably wide, studded with white sails, black funnels, little insects of skiffs, boats, rocky islands, and such like. Why need I describe it? When God Himself takes to panorama-painting, it turns out strangely beautiful. Few of my Switzerland reminiscences can compare to this; everything here looks so stern and robust, half enveloped in haze or smoke or fog.
[FMB]

It is beautiful here! In the evening a cool breeze is wafted from the sea, and then all objects appear clearly and sharply defined against the gray sky; the lights from the windows glitter brilliantly; so it was yesterday when I walked up and down the streets with Mr. Fergusson (an Edinburgh 'friend of mine', to whom Mr. Droop, a London 'friend of mine', has introduced me), and called at the post-office for your letter of the 13th inst. I read it with particular zest in Princes Street, Edinburgh. In Edinburgh, a letter from under the yew-tree in the Leipziger Strasse!
[FMB]

My swim in the sea was pleasant too today, and afloat on the waves I thought of you all, how very closely we are linked together, and yet I was in the deep Scotch ocean, that tastes very briny. Dobberan is lemonade compared to it.
[FMB]

Mendelssohn's letters from Edinburgh are restrictive in the topics they mention, but this is not surprising given that the duration of the travellers' stay in Edinburgh was only three days, and on one of these they journeyed out of town to meet Sir Walter Scott. It was natural therefore for Mendelssohn to confine himself to mentioning first impressions of the city and those aspects of its surroundings which particularly interested him; hill-walking and swimming in the sea were two of his favourite pastimes. Various other aspects of Edinburgh, its buildings and social life possibly attracted him, even if he did not have time to write about them.

In the years just prior to 1829 the City of Edinburgh had undergone a considerable physical transformation, and this had implications for the social structure of the town. As a visitor to the city before 1800 the traveller would have been impressed by the homeliness and neighbourliness of the Edinburgh citizens since Edinburgh in the late 1760s was like a small market town. There were wide differences of wealth and social rank, but there was very little separation of the social classes in terms of living accommodation.

Socially-acceptable places to stay, such as Milne's Court, were no more than a few hundred yards from unsavoury areas like the closes of Candlemaker Row. From the vantage point of a tenement window the scandal-monger could survey both the area round the Market Cross and the doors of the neighbouring drinking houses, and knew as much about the comings and goings, legal and illicit, of the socially elite as those of the working classes and the beggars.

Within a few years a new trend set in: the financially-better-off moved out from the High Street, some to George Square further south and others to the New Town on the north side of Princes Street. A degree of social mixing continued in the Old Town since lawyers and their clients still came to Parliament Hall off the High Street and undertook some of their affairs in

Edinburgh from the west end of Princes Street (1824)

the time-honoured way in the various taverns nearby, but the rich no longer
frequented the Old Town, simply sending their servants to the markets.
After 1800 shops and legal practices followed the drift of population away
from the Old Town, and some New Town dwellers hardly left the grandeur
of their spacious streets to frequent their former haunts in the High Street.
At the same time as these physical changes were taking place there also
occurred a change in the social behaviour of the people, and a more refined,
if less colourful, conduct replaced the coarse manners and open-hearted
warmth of the eighteenth century.

The nobility commonly lived in Edinburgh, but after 1815 it became more
usual to have a country residence, better transport making this reasonably
convenient. Literary circles and legal practices continued to flourish but the

leaders of society were now middle class, and in 1825 only two members of the nobility stayed permanently in Edinburgh.

It was a natural consequence of growth in Edinburgh for increasing attention to be paid to law enforcement, and Mendelssohn would not have been alone in noting the orderly behaviour of the citizens, at least by current standards. This situation was due mainly to the efficiency of the police, but it remained unsafe to go out on the streets of Edinburgh after darkness because of the gangs of youths which, after a few drinks in the taverns, roamed the streets; violent crime, however, was rather less common than Mendelssohn and Klingemann might have experienced in London or Glasgow

Mendelssohn probably would have been impressed by the cleanliness and general hygiene of Edinburgh – other than for the awful smell which occurred at ten o'clock each night as people removed the 'tub of nastiness' from each house. In the New Town, however, the density of population was much less and the sanitation arrangements more sophisticated. The growth in population required improved water supply, and there were frequently severe shortages which ended only in 1826 with the formation of the Edinburgh Joint Stock Water Company which initiated a new source of water supply from Crawley Springs. Mendelssohn enjoyed the recent innovation of a piped water supply although he missed the sight of the water-caddies who carried water in small casks (the charge was one penny a cask) from the public wells distributed around the main streets of the town.

Mendelssohn also benefited from the general improvement in standards of accommodation for visitors. Facilities of eighteenth-century Scottish inns ranged from basic to grim, but food supplies were always plentiful. The Lothians were one of the main arable areas of Scotland; vegetables were of high quality with lots of carrots and potatoes. The sea supported a highly productive fishing industry, and Edinburgh was as famous for its shellfish from the River Forth as for its strawberries which were available in very large quantities in the city during their brief season in July and August, which coincided with Mendelssohn's visit. More exotic imports were handled through the nearby port of Leith.

Goods were distributed to the people through the markets, the fish market and the flesh market being the most important. Situated under the North Bridge in 1829 these markets carried on their business in relatively unsanitary conditions, but prices even at current rates were a bargain: a penny for a good haddock, twopence for a dozen herring, and threepence for a lobster. Noisy haggling over prices was characteristic of the fish market, but the flesh

47

market was much quieter, the trade being run by a group of old women the majority of whom had succumbed to the ravages of gin and who sat on stools at stalls ranged round the Tron Church not far from the market.

Supper parties were typical of early nineteenth-century social life in Edinburgh, and the formal dinner with round after round of formal toasts was the social occasion for entertaining. Gradually the formality of such occasions declined, and friends could drop by for supper without prior invitation. Friendship and hospitality was widespread – but it had its drawbacks since drunkenness (perhaps witnessed by Mendelssohn) was the natural result of convivial gatherings. Edinburgh also had a very large number of clubs which met in the taverns of the city and 'tavern dissipation' was common to all social classes.

Had Mendelssohn's stay in Edinburgh been longer, he might have been tempted to undertake one of the many promenades into the country which was nearby, or have a round of golf on either Leith Links or Bruntsfield Links, or go horse racing at Musselburgh, or take part in a game of bowls.

A typical subject of conversation which Mendelssohn and Klingemann might have been involved in was the current scandal over the dire financial state of the City of Edinburgh, a topic which has a familiar ring even today. The city debt in 1789 was £168,982 and interest on the debt was paid by further borrowing. There were warnings that unless the city's finances were taken in hand and economies exercised in every department the administration would be taken out of the hands of the Magistrates and placed in the care of Trustees. Far from accepting cuts in expenditure, public works of an even greater scale than those of the eighteenth century were undertaken by the Town Council with a consequent further rise in the city debt. In 1819 a Committee of the House of Commons investigated the affairs of the Town Council and found that members did not understand the proper functioning of city finances, and indeed lacked interest in gaining a grasp of how to handle them correctly. Despite the incompetence underlined by the House of Commons Committee, the Magistrates continued their reckless spending, building the Royal High School in the mid-1820s on borrowed capital. A few years later the building of the western approach to the city involved them in borrowing much larger sums, but what finally brought to a head their insolvency was their scheme to enlarge Leith Docks. The docks at Leith provided revenue for Edinburgh Town Council, and the Council was aware that further capital investment would pay dividends in the long run. The big mistake they made was to borrow more money from the Government who, as creditors, initiated further investigations. These inquiries not only revealed

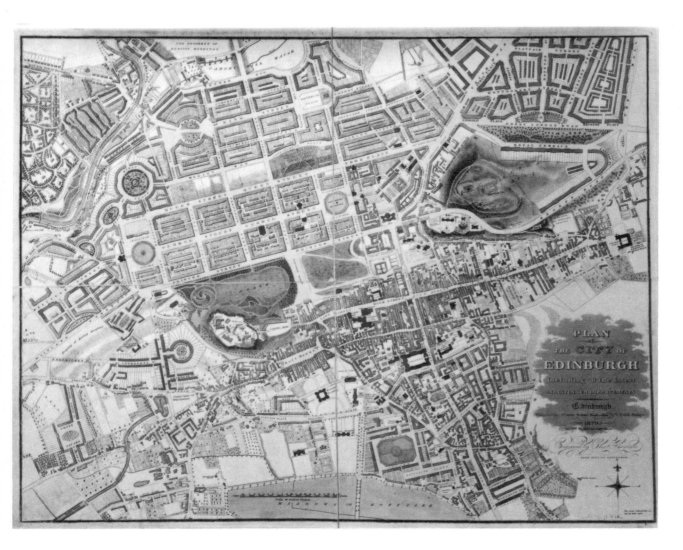

Section of Wood's map of Edinburgh (1820) showing the High Street, George Square and the New Town

a more or less bankrupt financial state but also provided material for gossip about the nature of expenditure:

Horse-race prizes and expenses   £668 per annum
Tavern expenses   £1,993 per annum
Lord Provost's salary   £500 per annum

49

Such figures make fantastic reading when one considers that it should have been possible to manage Edinburgh's entire local government for much less than £7,000 per annum. The debts of the city were not in question; rather the problem was how to settle them. Although Labouchère's report to the Chancellor of the Exchequer which recommended that creditors should receive a $2\frac{1}{4}\%$ return on sums owed them was not issued until 1836, and a final agreement giving 3% to creditors had to await a further two years, no doubt the whole topic of finance would have been a burning issue and matter of speculation at the time of Mendelssohn's visit.

Church-going throughout Edinburgh society was common, and not to attend church was frowned upon. As a consequence the church performed a unifying function on society and brought the rich and poor people into contact in a way that did not happen for the remainder of the week. It was natural on the occasion of a gathering of Highlanders for a bagpipes competition that Mendelssohn should notice them coming out of church:

> *Many Highlanders came in costume from church, victoriously leading their sweethearts in their Sunday attire, and casting magnificent and important looks over the world; with long red beards, tartan plaids, bonnets and feathers, naked knees, and their bagpipes in their hands, they passed quietly along by the half-ruined gray castle on the meadow, where Mary Stuart lived in splendour and saw Rizzio murdered. I feel as if the time went at a very rapid pace when I have before me so much that was and so much that is.*
> [FMB]

The sights and sounds of Edinburgh captured Mendelssohn's imagination, and the turbulent history of the capital acted as a background of experience against which he soon formed the idea of composing a Scottish symphony. On July 30, in the ruined chapel of Mary Stuart in the Palace of Holyrood, he composed the introduction to the first movement of a symphony and in a letter later wrote the following account of his visit to Holyrood House:

> *In the evening twilight we went today to the palace where Queen Mary lived and loved; a little room is shown there with a winding staircase leading up to the door; up this way they came and found Rizzio in that little room, pulled him out, and three rooms off there is a dark corner, where they murdered him. The chapel close to it is now roofless, grass and ivy grow there, and at that broken altar Mary was crowned Queen of Scotland.*

Everything round is broken and mouldering and the bright sky shines in. I believe I found today in that old chapel the beginning of my Scotch Symphony.
[FMB]

Though Mendelssohn began the composition of his 'Scotch' Symphony in 1829 he worked only intermittently on the piece and it was not completed until 1841, receiving its first performance in Leipzig in 1842.

A Visit to Abbotsford

Edinburgh: July 30, 1829

Beloved Ones, – It is late at night, and this is my last day in the town of Edinburgh. Tomorrow morning we go to Abbotsford to see Sir Walter Scott; the day after tomorrow, into the Highlands. The windows are open, for the weather is beautiful and the sky full of stars. Klingemann, in shirt sleeves, sits by my side writing.
[FMB]

Sir Walter Scott was born on August 15, 1771, in College Wynd, Edinburgh, youngest son of thirteen children, the first six of whom died as infants. His father was Walter Scott, a solicitor and Writer to the Signet, and shortly after Sir Walter's birth his parents moved to 25 George Square. This move was typical of the current trend to move out from the High Street to the more socially-acceptable areas of the New Town and George Square. When he was eighteen months old young Walter had a serious illness which left him lame for life. Sir Walter was educated at the High School, and the University of Edinburgh, and after studying law he became an advocate (the Scottish equivalent of a barrister). He married Margaret Charlotte Charpentier in 1797, and after their marriage the young couple lived partly in Edinburgh and partly at Lasswade Cottage, just south of Edinburgh. In 1802 they bought 39 Castle Street which remained their Edinburgh home until 1826 when Sir Walter had to sell it owing to his financial difficulties. Sir Walter was made Sheriff-Depute of Selkirkshire in 1799 and soon found it essential to have a house nearer to his work than Lasswade. He moved in 1804 to Ashiestiel, on the river Tweed six miles above Abbotsford. King George IV created a baronetcy for Sir Walter in 1820.

From his childhood and many rides on horseback into the Border valleys of Ettrick, Teviot, Tweed and Yarrow Sir Walter felt a deep love of this countryside. His lease of Ashiestiel which he rented from his cousins was coming to an end, and he decided to become a Tweedside landowner by buying up a farm for 4,000 guineas on the right bank of the Tweed. The purchase took place in 1811, and his money bought uncultivated ground covered with heath totalling one hundred and ten acres. His family moved to their new house in 1812 and, as the land had once belonged to the monks of

53

Melrose and a ford across the river just below the house had been used by the monks, he decided to change the name of the property from the original Cartley-hole to Abbotsford. Plans for enlarging the house were already in his mind when Sir Walter and his family moved into Abbotsford, but the additional building, consisting of an armoury, dining room, study, conservatory and three upstairs bedrooms, was not carried out until six years later, in 1818.

It was at Abbotsford that he began the *Waverley* novels, the first of which gave the series its title, and from the financial success of his writings he was able to indulge his desire to enlarge his estate and to further extend Abbotsford. In 1822 the old farmhouse was entirely demolished to be replaced by the present main block of Abbotsford. Sir Walter occupied the new house in the autumn of 1824, and it was in these new buildings that Mendelssohn and Klingemann visited the author.

Mendelssohn and Klingemann entered Abbotsford by the South Court, the east side of which is formed by a stone screen copied from the cloisters at Melrose Abbey which they had passed on their journey from Edinburgh. In the south wall of the court are five medallions from the old Cross of Edinburgh, and in the same wall are set, alternating with the medallions, six rectangular stones from the Roman camp at Old Penrith. A fountain, of which the bowl was once part of the Mercat Cross in Edinburgh, stands in the centre of the court. To the right of the entrance porch is a horse mounting block in the form of a stone statue of Sir Walter's deerhound, Maida; the statue was sculpted by John Smith in 1824 and later that year the dog died and was buried beneath it. The condemned criminals' door from the old Tolbooth of Edinburgh which was pulled down in 1817 is set into the upper wall of the house, to the left of the entrance. In the Tolbooth this door led out on to a flat roof where stood the scaffold, and it is incorporated into the structure of Abbotsford so that it again leads out on to a flat roof.

From the South Court the visitors went into the Entrance Hall, the walls of which are lined partly with ornately carved panels from the Auld Kirk of Dunfermline and partly with plain oak panelling from the same church. Like the stone screen outside, the carving of the stone fireplace is partly copied from Melrose Abbey, in this case from one of the stalls in the cloisters. No doubt proud of his historical acquisitions, Sir Walter could well have pointed out the old basket grate, believed to have been the property of Archbishop Sharp who was murdered on Magus Muir in 1679, two cannon balls which were said to have been fired at the siege of Roxburgh Castle in 1460, and a copy of the skull of Robert the Bruce made when his tomb was opened in 1818 at Dunfermline.

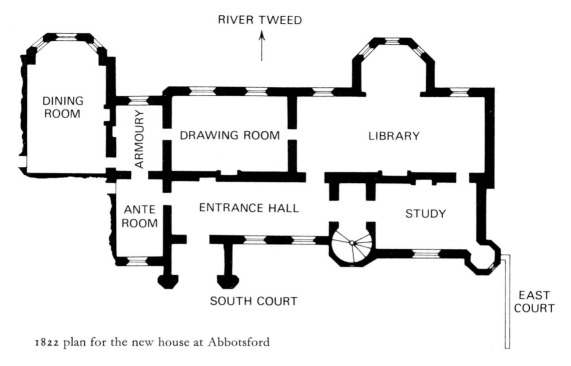

RIVER TWEED

DINING ROOM

ARMOURY

DRAWING ROOM

LIBRARY

ANTE ROOM

ENTRANCE HALL

STUDY

SOUTH COURT

EAST COURT

1822 plan for the new house at Abbotsford

Abbotsford from a vantage point overlooking the South Court

55

Sir Walter Scott, from original by J. P. Knight

Abbotsford: July 31, 1829

*Most astonished friends! O most amazed readers! Under us the great man
is snoring, his dogs are asleep and his armoured knights awake: it is
twelve o'clock, and the sweetest ghostly hour which I have ever spent, for
Miss Scott makes the most delicious marmalade – the trees of the park are
rustling, the waves of the Tweed whisper to the bard the tales of long
bygone days, and the mystery of the present; and harp-strains, sounded by
tender hands, mingle therewith, vibrating through the strange old-fashioned
apartment in which our celebrated host has quartered us. Never was a letter
begun with greater relish, and we look down very much on Europe. When
this morning at a quarter to six we drove out of Edinburgh, still quite
sleepy, strange sounds fell on our ears: the stage was already in motion,
I rushed on to catch it, a street-porter (here of course a Highlander)
stopped it and called out eagerly, 'Run, my man, run, my man; it won't
wait!' What signify another forty miles, if then we discover the sources of
the Nile? We were in Melrose: Felix drove to Abbotsford; I stayed
behind, as a person without a letter of introduction, who might follow if Sir
Walter would positively not let the other go. Melrose Abbey is a ruin full
of preservation and conversation; King David (of Scotland) and the magician
Scott (Michael, not Walter) are there cut in stone, and the whole neighbourhood is interwoven with legends and ancient fairy dances. Thomas the
Rhymer and the Fairy Queen held their revels a little higher up in the dark
glen, and something of that still animates the castellan when he scrambles like
a chamois up to the highest point of the ruins. One gets so hungry in such ruins
(which by way of contrast throw the present in one's very face)
that I retired into the inn for bread and cheese and ale and a
newspaper. So I lay in quiet enjoyment on the sofa, when the coach came
back and some one rushed into our room. Thinking only of Felix, I made
some scurrilous remark. That moment I discerned an elderly man: 'Oh
Sir Walter!' cried I, jumping up; and with apologizing blushes I added,
'Familiar likenesses can alone excuse like familiarity!' 'Never mind!' was his
brief reply – he who is so famed for prolixity! 'My dear future Parnassus-
brother and historical novelist, I have much pleasure in meeting you. Your
friend has already beautifully told me what and how much you will yet
write and may have written.' Meanwhile hands were shaken out of joint
and shaken in again, and we all proceeded in happy ecstasy to Abbotsford.
This very evening Felix and I tremblingly wrote music and verses in a large
album. I wrote the following:*

57

Hohe Berge steigen himmelaufwärts
Und die Moore liegen rabenschwaiz dazwischen,
Felsen, Schluchten, Schlösser, Trümmer reden von uralter
     Vergangenheit,
Und sinnverwirrend umrauscht es die Neuen,
Die davon träumen, ohne es zu verstehn.
Aber an den Pforten des Landes wohnt Einer,
Der, ein Weiser, der Rathsel kundig ist
Und der alles Alte neu an's Licht bringt –
Nun ziehen die Frohen
Und rauschen und lauschen
Und reisen und weisen
Verstehen und sehen
Die Felsen und Schluchten und Schlösser und Trümmer.
Der Weise aber hebet noch immer die Schatze
Und munzt sie ein in goldne, klingende Batzen!
         Dies zum Andenken von etc. etc.

[CK]

[Lofty mountains rising to the skies,
Raven-black moors far between expanding,
Rocks, crevices, castles, ruins, speak of the primaeval past,
In magic rustle sweeping by the living,
Who dream of it, but cannot understand it.
But at the gates of that old land there lives one,
A sage, who has the knowledge of those riddles,
And brings to fresh new light the wan old darkness –
Now come all the gay,
And listen and stay,
And travel and revel,
Delight in the sight,
Of the rocks and the crevices, castles and ruins,
But the sage evermore he digs up hidden treasures,
Coining silver and gold, spreading wondrous fair pleasures.
        This in remembrance of, etc. (trans. C. Klingemann)]

P.S. – This is all Klingemann's invention. We found Sir Walter in the act of
leaving Abbotsford, stared at him like fools, drove eighty miles and lost a
day for the sake of at best one half-hour of superficial conversation. Melrose

compensated us but little: we were out of humour with great men, with ourselves, with the world, with everything. It was a bad day. To-day, however, was glorious! We have forgotten the ills of yesterday, and can laugh over them.

[FMB]

The Highland Journey

Edinburgh: July 28, 1829

The Highland journey will be as follows: via Stirling, Perth, Dunkeld, and the waterfalls to Blair Athol; thence on foot over the hills to Inveraray, to Glencoe, the Isle of Staffa, and the Isle of Islay; there a stay of several days will be made, because Sir Alexander Johnston has sent after me a letter of introduction to Sir Walter Campbell, the Lord, owner, and tyrant of the island, whom a word of Johnston's tames and turns into a willing guide. From there up the Clyde to Glasgow, then to Ben Lomond, which with Loch Lomond forms the Highland lion, to Loch Earn, Ben Voirlich [Vorlich], Loch Katrine; then to Cumberland. What further shall I tell you? Time and space are coming to an end, and everything must terminate, in the refrain 'How kind the people are in Edinburgh, and how generous is the good God.' The Scotch ladies also deserve notice, and if Mahmud follows father's advice and turns Christian, I shall in his place become a Turk and settle in this neighbourhood.
[FMB]

This proposed itinerary for their Scottish Highland journey, set out in one of Mendelssohn's letters written from Edinburgh, varies in some details from the tour which they actually undertook, and on page 62 you will see a map indicating those places which Mendelssohn and Klingemann did visit according to later letters written during the course of their sojourn.

Mendelssohn and Klingemann were undertaking their Highland journey by means of a coaching system which was much more recent in its establishment than that which had brought them to the Scottish capital. The great political and social changes of the period following the unsuccessful Jacobite Rebellion of 1745 had left the country in a state of poverty and peace. Growing interest in Scottish affairs brought about an influx of economists, farmers, and social workers who improved standards of farming and achieved a measure of industrial development. Thomas Telford, working for the Commissioners for Highland Roads and Bridges, opened up Highland communications in the early years of the nineteenth century. The coach service by which Mendelssohn and Klingemann travelled from Edinburgh to Stirling in 1829 had been in operation for only twenty-two years. This route

Map of Highland Journey
From their letters it is difficult to trace the travellers' route from Loch Eck to Glasgow, but one possibility is that they travelled overland from Loch Eck to the small port of Kilmun from which a packet steamer left for Glasgow.

62

served the towns of Linlithgow and Falkirk. After Stirling the coach travelled to Perth via Dunblane and Crieff.

Birnam: August 2, 1829

Mendelssohn: Birnam Wood near Dunkeld

Dunkeld: August 2, 1829

Mendelssohn: the Rumbling Bridge near Dunkeld

Blair Athol: August 3, 1829

This is a most dismal, melancholy, rainy day. But we make shift as best we can, which indeed is not saying much. Earth and sky are wet through,

and whole regiments of clouds are still marching up. Yesterday was a lovely day, we passed from rock to rock, many waterfalls, beautiful valleys, with rivers, dark woods and heath with the red heather in blossom. In the morning we drove in an open carriage, and then walked twenty-one (English) miles. I sketched a great deal, and Klingemann hit upon the divine idea, which I am sure will give you great pleasure, of writing some rhymes at every spot of which I make a sketch. Yesterday and to-day we have been carrying out the plan, which answers charmingly; he has already composed very pretty things.
[FMB]

Bridge of Tummel: August 3, 1829 (evening)

A wild affair! The storm howls, rushes, and whistles, doors are banging and the window-shutters are bursting open. Whether the watery noise is from the driving rain or the foaming stream there's no telling, as both rage together; we are sitting here quietly by the fire, which I poke from time to time to make it flare up. The room is large and empty, from one of the walls the wet trickles down, the floor is so thin that the conversation from the servants' room below penetrates up to us: they are singing drunken songs and laughing: dogs are barking. We have two beds with crimson curtains; on our feet, instead of English slippers, are Scotch wooden shoes; tea with honey and potato cakes; there is a wooden winding staircase, on which the servant-girl came to meet us with whisky, a desperate cloud-procession in the sky, and in spite of the servants' noise and door-banging there is repose. It is quiet and very lonely here! I might say that the stillness rings through the noise. Just now the door opens of itself. This is a Highland inn. The little boys with their kilts and bare knees and gay-coloured bonnets, the waiter in his tartan, old people with pigtails, talk helter-skelter in their unintelligible Gaelic.
[FMB]

Following Mendelssohn's description of a Highland inn the remainder of the letter describes the countryside north of Pitlochry and his attempts to capture the distinctive character of the scenery.

The country is far and wide thickly overgrown with foliage, from all sides ample water is rushing from under the bridges, there is little corn, much heather brown and red, precipices, passes, crossways, beautiful green every-

*where, deep-blue water – but all stern, dark, very lonely. But why describe it?
Ask Droysen, he knows it better, and can paint it: we have been
constantly repeating lines from his 'Hochlands' to each other. Dear Droysen,
how is it that you know Scotland? It is just as you describe it.*

*This evening I am reading the 'Flegeljahre', and my sisters are looking
at me wistfully.* [*Felix's sisters had sent to him in England Jean Paul's
Flegeljahre in which Hensel (Mendelssohn's future brother-in-law) had
drawn their portraits as a frontspiece.*] *Hensel understands his business:
he knows how to see faces and how to fix them. But the weather is discouraging.*

*I have invented a new manner of drawing on purpose for it, and have rubbed
in clouds today and painted grey mountains with my pencil. Klingemann is
rhyming briskly, and I finish my sketches during the rain.*
[FMB]

Falls of Moness: August 4, 1829

Mendelssohn: Falls of Moness, Birks of Aberfeldy

Loch Tay: August 5, 1829

Ben More: August 5, 1829

Mendelssohn: the foot of Ben More

From Klingemann's letter of August 7 we learn that he and Mendelssohn made their way via Fort William and Oban to Tobermory where they rested in preparation for their trip to Staffa and Iona planned for the following day.

67

The youngsters of Tobermory, the capital of the Isle of Mull, are merrily bustling by the harbour, the Atlantic Ocean, which appears to contain abundance of water, is quietly riding at anchor, the same as our steamer; we have found quarters in a respectable private house, and would willingly leave a memorial of our day's work in always issuing, like Napoleon, our army-bulletins from places of note. Perfectly charming it is here! From my earliest days I have confounded the Hebrides with the Hesperides; and if we did not find the oranges on the trees, they lay at least in the whisky-toddy. Yesterday we moved up-hill and down-hill, our cart generally rolling on by the side, and we ourselves stalking onwards through heather and moors and all kinds of passes (nature here is so amply provided with them that Government does not ask for any ['Pass' is the German word for passport]), under clouds, and in a thick drizzling rain, through the Highlands. Smoky huts were stuck on cliffs, ugly women looked through the window-holes, cattle-herds with Rob Roys now and then blocked up the way, mighty mountains were sticking up to their knees (the latter in Highland costume) in the clouds, and looked out again from the top, but we often saw little. Late last night we unexpectedly stumbled upon a bit of culture again, viz. the one street of which Fort William consists, and this morning we embraced the very newest piece of culture, steam, and were again among many people, greedily enjoying sunshine and sea-green, the wide outlines of the sea, the rocks at modest distance, good cheer, and society of all kinds. A new friend told us at once that yonder young couple were on their honeymoon excursion, and that he had seen them on Ben Lomond shortly after the wedding dance a Scotch reel, the bride with parting tears in her eyes. By the harbour of Oban Bruce's Rock rises up, where he is said to have done some great deed or other; the Laird MacDonald goes home with his ladies to a new house, which stands behind the ruins of the old castle, and where a silver brooch of Bruce's is still kept; our Edinburgh friend, Captain Nelson of the Navy, with whom we met on the ship and shook hands with, tells us wonderful stories of how this relic had once been lost and bought again at a high price, and that once it was stolen along with other things, and at last found in possession of a lady-descendant of Rob Roy.
[CK]

Oban: August 7, 1829

The view towards the Hebrides dated August 7 was the inspiration of the

Mendelssohn: view towards the Hebrides. Mendelssohn and Klingemann made two copies of the record of their journey in sketches and verses, a fact which probably accounts for the unfinished state of some of the drawings, including this view towards the Hebrides. (Klingemann's copy is now in Sweden, and Mendelssohn's copy was bequeathed to his granddaughter, Miss M. D. M. Benecke. Her copy was given to the Bodleian Library, Oxford, by her friend Miss M. E. Andrews, to whom Miss Benecke had left it in her will.)

overture later called *Fingal's Cave*, the opening music of which is quoted in Mendelssohn's letter of the same date.

Hebrides: August 7, 1829

In order to make you understand how extraordinarily the Hebrides affected me, the following came into my mind there:

In *Mendelssohn, Letters and Recollections* (transl. M. E. von Glehn. London, 1872) Dr Ferdinand Hiller remembered talking to the composer about *The Hebrides* Overture in the following terms:

> *Mendelssohn had brought with him to Paris the draught-score of the 'Hebrides' Overture. He told me that not only was its general form and colour suggested to him by the sight of Fingal's Cave, but that the first few bars, containing the principal subject, had actually occurred to him on the spot. The same evening he and his friend Klingemann paid a visit to a Scotch family. There was a piano in the drawing-room, but being Sunday, music was utterly out of the question, and Mendelssohn had to employ all his diplomacy to get the instrument opened for a single minute, so that he and Klingemann might hear the theme which forms the germ of that original and masterly Overture.*

This account conflicts with the evidence of Mendelssohn's letter of August 7 in which he notes the theme which occurred to him as a result of the impression which the Hebrides made upon him, and, in any case, Mendelssohn and Klingemann did not visit Fingal's Cave until August 8. This throws into doubt the long-accepted assumption that the sight of Fingal's Cave was the inspiration for the opening bars of Mendelssohn's Opus 26.

The uninhabited island of Staffa lies seven miles off the west coast of Mull. The derivation of the name is Norse (Staffa meaning Stave Island) and the Norsemen built their stave houses with tree logs set vertical like the columnar basalt of the walls of the cave. The island is less than a mile long, and the cliffs which rise from 50 to 135 feet are riddled by caves. At the south point of the island is Fingal's Cave which is seventy-six yards deep and sixty-six

Fingal's Cave from the sea

feet high. The columns of black pillars at Fingal's Cave are almost perfectly symmetrical, and on the left-hand wall they rise to forty feet.

Fingal was the Scottish form of the name Fionn MacCoul, a famous Celtic warrior whose life was devoted to driving the Norsemen out of the islands off the west coast of Scotland called the Hebrides. The Scottish name Fingal was derived from the Gaelic Fionn na Ghal (Chief of Valour).

71

Impressions of Fingal's Cave

The English poet Keats (who visited the island ten years before Mendelssohn) wrote:

> *Suppose, now, the giants who came down to the daughters of men had taken a whole mass of these columns and bound them together like bunches of matches, and then with immense axes had made a cavern in the body of these columns. Such is Fingal's Cave, except that the sea has done the work of excavation and is continually dashing there. The colour of the columns is a sort of black, with a lurking gloom of purple therein. For solemnity and grandeur it far surpasses the finest cathedral.*

Sir Walter Scott also wrote of Staffa:

> *The shores of Mull on the eastward lay,*
> *And Ulva dark and Colonsay,*
> *And all the group of islets gay*
> *   That guard famed Staffa round.*
> *Then all unknown its columns rose,*
> *Where dark and undisturbed repose*
> *   the cormorant had found,*
> *And the shy seal had quiet home,*
> *And weltered in that wondrous dome,*
> *Where Nature herself, it seemed, would raise*
> *A Minster to her Maker's praise!*
> *Not for a meaner use ascend*
> *Her columns, or her arches bend;*
> *Nor of a theme less solemn tells*
> *That mighty surge that ebbs and swells.*
> *And still, between each awful pause*
> *From the high vault an answer draws.*

Sea-trip: August 8, 1829

The following account of their trip to Staffa and Iona is taken from a letter by Klingemann dated August 10, written from Glasgow.

> *On the said early morning, the agreeable steam-persons, who at first came flying*

towards us with nothing but olive-leaves, became lower and lower, the more the barometer sank and the sea rose. For that the Atlantic did, it stretched its thousand feelers more and more roughly, twirling us about like anything. The ship-household kept its breakfast almost for itself, few people on board being able to manage their cups and saucers, ladies as a rule fell down like flies, and one or the other gentleman followed their example; I only wish my travelling fellow-sufferer had not been among them, but he is on better terms with the sea as a musician than as an individual or a stomach; two beautiful cold daughters of a Hebrides aristocrat, at whom Felix may storm, quietly continued sitting on deck, and did not even care much for the sea-sickness of their own mother. Also there sat placidly by the steam-engine, warming herself in the cold wind, a woman of two-and-eighty. That woman has six times touched me and seven times irritated me. She wanted to see Staffa before her end. Staffa, with its strange basalt pillars and caverns, is in all picture-books. We were put out in boats and lifted by the hissing sea up the pillar stumps to the celebrated Fingal's Cave. A greener roar of waves surely never rushed into a stranger cavern – its many pillars making it look like the inside of an immense organ, black and resounding, and absolutely without purpose, and quite alone, the wide gray sea within and without. There the old woman scrambled about laboriously, close to the water: she wanted to see the cave of Staffa before her end, and she saw it. We returned in the little boat to our steamer, to that unpleasant steam-smell. When the second boat arrived, I could see with what truth at the theatre they represent the rising and falling of a boat, when the hero saves the heroine out of some trouble. There was a certain comfort in seeing that the two aristocratic faces had after all turned pale, as I looked at them through my black eye-glass. The two-and-eighty-years-old woman was also in the boat trembling, the boat went up and down, with difficulty she was lifted out – but she had seen Staffa before her end. The pleasure increased in gravity; where yesterday nice conversation went on, to-day silence was indulged in. The glossy negro, yesterday on deck, who (when he did not smoke) played on tambourine and pipe the Huntsmen's Chorus on the Atlantic, and who in the evening had all the juveniles of Tobermory in his train, had remained there. The yellow mulatto cook, whose shining Caliban-countenance we joyfully watched yesterday amongst saucepans, herrings and vegetables, was now frying some stale ham, the smell of which drove some suffering navigators to despair, if not worse; the surviving passengers conspired against the captain, who, to oblige Sir James, was going to sail back by the roundabout way, instead of taking the short cut by Iona to Oban. Iona, one of the Hebrides-sisters – there is truly a very Ossianic

and sweetly sad sound about that name – when in some future time I shall
sit in a madly crowded assembly with music and dancing round me, and the
wish arises to retire into the loneliest loneliness, I shall think of Iona with
its ruins of a once magnificent cathedral, the remains of a convent, the graves
of ancient Scotch kings and still more ancient northern pirate-princes –
with their ships rudely carved on many a monumental stone. If I had my
home on Iona, and lived there upon melancholy as other people do on their
rents, my darkest moment would be when in that wide space, that deals
in nothing but cliffs and sea-gulls, suddenly a curl of steam should appear,
followed by a ship and finally by a gay party in veils and frock-coats,
who would look for an hour at the ruins and graves and the three little
huts for the living, and then move off again. This highly unjustifiable joke,
occurring twice a week, and being almost the only thing to make one aware
that there are such things as time and clocks in the world, would be as if the
inhabitants of those old graves haunted the place in a ludicrous disguise.
Opposite Iona stands a rocky island, which, to complete the effect, looks like
a ruined city.

Gradually the sea-sick people recovered, a sail was spread, by way of tent,
on deck, less for keeping off the sun than the wet, which is a constant matter
of dispute between Felix and me, since he calls it rain, and I call it mist;
we kept open table in the face of all the sea-monsters of the Atlantic; even
Felix fell to and stood out like his own self; Sir James took wine with
those that had not complained of him – we refraining from that honour.
At seven o'clock in the evening we ought to have been back in Oban, our
continent, but we only reached Tobermory; some of the party went on shore,
the negro did not entice the insular juveniles, for it rained, and he would not
have found favour. Night came on, the captain coolly cast anchor in some
corner or other, and we lay down in the cabin; beds there were none, and
herrings are lodged in spacious halls compared to us. At times when half
asleep I tried to drive away flies from my face, and then found they were
the grizzly locks of the old Scotchman; if the Pope had been amongst us, some
Protestant might unawares have kissed his slipper, for we often chanced to
make unknown boots act as pillows. It was a wild night's revel without
the merry cup, and with rain and wind for the boisterous songsters.

Mendelssohn cannot altogether have enjoyed seeing Fingal's Cave since
he was so violently seasick. However, the island of Staffa and the Atlantic
rollers made a profound impression on him, and when he returned to Germany
he developed the musical sketch on page 70 into an overture called *The*
Lonely Island, later re-written and given a new name – *The Hebrides*. When the

piece was published Mendelssohn was persuaded to give it the alternative title of *Fingal's Cave*.

The main tune with which the overture begins pictures the gentle ebb and flow of the tide washing into Fingal's Cave, and after some music suggesting the Atlantic breakers beating on the shores of the 'lonely island', we hear a broad, surging melody for 'cellos. These two themes, the first based on short rhythmic motives and the second a singing melody, form the basis of Mendelssohn's musical material for his overture.

The Hebrides Overture is a masterpiece of delicate and effective orchestration, but, further than this, Wagner described the overture as an 'aquarelle' by a great landscape-painter. Today we regard the harmonic and instrumental effects of the piece as a model of clarity, but it was not so regarded at its first performance: 'indirectness', 'veiled effects on trumpets', trumpets sounding as if played 'through a curtain of water' – these were the terms in which the music was being discussed. Similar semi-critical words were being used to describe the indistinctiveness and coalesced forms and colour schemes in Turner's contemporary oil-painting *Staffa, Fingal's Cave*. Indeed, the dissatisfied buyer of Turner's painting complained that the picture was 'indistinct', to which the artist replied, 'Indistinctness is my forte.'

Turner had followed an almost identical Highland journey to that of Mendelssohn, and the fact that the two works share a measure of vagueness in interpreting the Scottish seascape is more than coincidental. Turner's treatment of the sea on canvas is the equivalent of Mendelssohn's musical interpretation of the forces of Nature, and not of his sketches. In Romantic painting of the nineteenth century, subject matter was of major importance, and much of the concern of contemporary artists was directed towards the search for appropriate themes and the means of interpreting these; their concern was to express ideas and to lay less emphasis on the form which this expression might take. This is not to say that form is not important in Romantic painting, but that subject matter was at least equally important. The link between the violence of Mendelssohn's storm sequence in the 'Fingal's Cave' Overture and themes in contemporary Romantic art is clearly put by T. S. R. Boase in *Journal of the Warburg and Courtauld Institutes* (Volume 22, 1960) in which he discusses Romantic subject matter.

> *The revolt of the romantics at the close of the eighteenth and beginning of the nineteenth centuries demonstrated itself in a choice of subjects hitherto held below the dignity of high art, either from periods considered barbaric, incidents thought to be unrestrained and sensational, or from the contemporary scene. It was a breaking of bounds in which extremes had a value of their*

own as such, and agony and physical suffering were eagerly portrayed in defiance of classical nobility and reserve. . . Topics that had hitherto been relegated to popular engravings or prints began to be used for serious art, and the horrible and shocking became, as in some twentieth century movements, enlightened and advanced. . . Of all contemporary nightmares that of shipwreck was one of the most obsessing.

The theme of shipwreck was especially important to artists in Britain because of the number of disasters at sea. Mendelssohn would have been aware that circa 1800 approximately five thousand Britons per year perished at sea. Relative to the population's size which, according to the 1801 census, was ten-and-a-half million, the figures for those lost at sea are significant. Shipwreck and the fickle moods of the sea which becalms or storm-tosses ships at her whim were also important subjects in Romantic poetry where they take on an additional meaning: the storm-tossed boat is a symbol of the distressed individual battling against the forces of the universe. In literature Medieval subjects and Nordic legends were exploited for their menacing qualities; Scotland was the home of the third-century Gaelic poet, Ossian, the son of Fingal, and a collection of his 'Ancient Epic Poems' was first translated and published by James Macpherson in 1760. The demand for such literature in the early nineteenth century may be measured by the extent to which Ossian was featured in the literature and painting of the Romantic period, and this in spite of the fact that it was revealed in the late eighteenth century that Ossian was a figment of the imagination of the dishonest Mr Macpherson. It is interesting to speculate on the extent to which fake mythology acted as an inspiration to Romantic artists.

Turner's paintings were frequently allied to a piece of poetry, sometimes written by himself, and usually printed in the exhibition catalogue as part of the description of the picture. Klingemann's verses inscribed on Mendelssohn's sketches form an interesting parallel to Turner's practice. This mixture of literary and visual images was an attempt to let the effects of each art impinge on the other. Turner's quotations deal generally with the atmospheric effects pictured in his works, and after the year 1798 poetry regularly appeared in the Royal Academy catalogues. *Slave Ship* by Turner was based on a newspaper account of the horrors of the slave trade and on part of James Thomson's poem *Summer*, a piece based on the same theme.

Increasing still the terror of these storms,
His jaws horrific arm'd with threefold fate,
Here dwells the direful shark. Lur'd by the scent

William Turner: *Staffa, Fingal's Cave* (1832)

Of steaming crowds, of rank disease, and death,
Behold! He rushing cuts the briny flood,
Swift as the gale can bear the ship along;
And from the partners of that cruel trade
Which spoils unhappy Guinea of her sons,
Demands his share of prey – demands themselves.

The language of this poem is full of Romantic extravagance and surprisingly pre-dates Klingemann's efforts in the same style (see p. 58) by a century. A tendency towards the merging of form and meaning which

77

John Flaxman: *Ulysses slaying the Suitors* (1793)

Eugène Delacroix: *Apollo slaying Python* (1849)

characterises Lessing's *Nathan the Wise* conflicted with the Classicist's desire to retain clarity of expression, and this has an exact equivalent in painting and drawing. The divergence of style between the neo-classic drawings of the English sculptor, John Flaxman (1755–1826) on the one hand and the indistinctness of outline of the drawings of Delacroix on the other is vividly demonstrated in the following two examples of their work.

It is in this context that we can see the draughtsmanship of Mendelsshon's sketches following an established tradition of the nineteenth century. It is perhaps important not to confuse Mendelssohn's sketching style with a tendency which resulted from a certain antipathy to formal training amongst later Romantic artists which meant that they remained technically incompetent if not simply ignorant about some of the more difficult techniques of painting; the sketchiness which resulted was not merely the style of the non-professional but was a consequence of the artist's longing to set down his first thoughts with freedom and flexibility.

To Glasgow

After the grandeur of their Hebrides experience Mendelssohn and Klingemann set off on the journey from Oban to Inveraray.

At half past six on Sunday morning we landed at Oban in the rain. Not wishing to hear a Gaelic sermon, we mounted one of those eligible open vehicles that are called carts, 'sheltered' by the rain: at last, however, the sun came out, warming our hearts and drying our cloaks.
[CK]

Inveraray: August 9, 1829

In Inveraray we found an excellent inn and good quarters. Our host's beautiful daughter in her black curls looked out like a sign over the signboard into the harbour, in which the newest herrings are swimming about all alive at nine o'clock in the morning, and at a quarter past nine are served up fried with the coffee. Sympathising fellow-travellers eased our minds of our past sufferings and our feet of our torn boots. The Duke of Argyll's castle proudly looked forth from between the lofty trees; and from the tops of the surrounding hills the green trees held a colloquy with their relations below, who were already appointed to the navy and swam about in the water.
[CK]

The journey from Inveraray to Glasgow

Our longing for culture and letters drove us to Glasgow by a wondrous road through divers 'lochs' (i.e. lakes) and some land. Out of a steamboat on which we embarked, whilst our host's black-curled daughter thumped the piano, we were to have been transferred into a steam-coach, but our locomotion was effected by horses, and the former vehicle stood idly by the road-side, having already been used but not found quite practicable yet, and looking very ridiculous with a high funnel and a rudder. Then we were again lodged in a steamboat, which was said to be of iron: the walls, however, at which we knocked were of wood. Then again we drove a little

81

*distance on land, until we came to Loch Hech [Eck], there once more got on
board a steamer, which finally delivered us to a final one in the mouth of the
Clyde, and we sailed up the Clyde to Glasgow: a splendid sail, scarcely
any waves, watering-places on the river with large vessels, sea-gulls, steamers
fast gliding past, villas, a rock with Dumbarton Castle and a view of the
clear wide distance, and the blue towering magnificent Ben Lomond.*

*We saw him [Ben Lomond] for the first time. The country became more
flat, and soft corn-fields gave us a familiar greeting like old acquaintances,
after our long roaming along the proud and silent mountains. Everything
was still and peaceful. Three kinds of stillnesses are here: between the*

82

mountains the water rushes, but it is sternly still; in the sea between the islands the waves roll, but it is dismally still; in the smooth water the steam-boats fly, but it is mildly and recreatively still. The first are wild fellows, who refuse learning and working; the second are discharged gods, who are sulking; the last are good children after a good day's work.
[CK]

Impressions of Glasgow

In Glasgow there are seventy steam-boats, forty of which start every day, and many long chimneys are smoking. An excellent inn refreshes us; the waiters minister to us with two hands and as many feet, as steam-service in hotels has not yet been invented.
[CK]

Sitting, as we are now, in the best hotel of a commercial town of 160,000 inhabitants, which has a university and cotton manufactories, and coffee and sugar at first hand, we look back with equanimity on past disasters: the Highlands, however, and the sea brew nothing but whisky and bad weather. Here it is different and smooth, but comfortable. With a blue sky overhead, and a good sofa underneath, palatable victuals before and ministering spirits around us, we brave all dangers, particularly the past ones.
[CK]

We have seen and admired Glasgow. This morning we were in a stupendous cotton mill, as full of maddening noise as the divine waterfall of Monass. What is the difference to the ear? One old work-woman wore a wreath of cotton, another had tied up her aching tooth with it. Hundreds of little girls toil there from their earliest days and look yellow. But there will ever exist poetry about it. Systematic order becomes sublime, and the whole swallows itself up in succession, like seasons and vegetation. I joke little and admire much.
[CK]

The travellers disembarked from their steamer a little distance down river from the Broomielaw, and their first sight of Glasgow would have been very very similar to that pictured by Joseph Swan.

With the coming of the Industrial Revolution Glasgow's population leapt from forty thousand to two hundred thousand between the years 1780 and 1830. As visitors, Mendelssohn and Klingemann could not but have been impressed by the way in which the town had completely overrun its former boundaries; within fifty years there had been an enormously rapid growth of streets, buildings and people, and the new buildings followed certain directions depending on the availability of land for purchase and on its

85

Joseph Swan: The Broomielaw (circa 1825)

suitability for building. The newest buildings sprung up in the west of
Glasgow, and the building around George Square housing the Post Office
and Municipal Buildings became the centre of the city. Elegant residential
houses lined the streets leading off George Square where such industrial
barons as the brothers W. and J. Coats, the cotton-thread manufacturers,
stayed. The other main direction of growth which Mendelssohn and his
companion would have noted was the development over the River Clyde
adjacent to the little village of Gorbals.

The main industry of Glasgow in 1829 was textile manufacture and the
smoking chimneys of the factories dominated the skyline. It came naturally to
a city used to overseas trade to transform an imported raw material, cotton,

86

into good-quality fabrics, and then to ship most of these again to European and American markets. The first experiments in textile manufacture were limited in scale and sometimes unusual in concept; a power loom was devised to be operated by a Newfoundland dog walking round and round inside a treadmill, but Richard Arkwright's looms driven by water-power soon put an end to such cruelty. By the end of the Napoleonic Wars the Corporation of Glasgow had to regulate the numbers of steam engines which operated in the city's mills by means of a private Act of Parliament because smoke was beginning to constantly blanket the city and was recognised as a pollution hazard. By 1820 there were fifty steam-powered mills in Glasgow, and production was forty times greater than just twenty years previously. Napoleon's blockade of British ports gave opportunities to ambitious individuals to make vast sums illegally by smuggling, a challenge which the Finlay family, associated with the marketing of cotton textiles, eagerly took up by establishing a trading post at Heligoland.

The stimulus given to local engine-building works by the textile manufacturers established an industry which supplied machines for collieries to the east of Glasgow and engines for steamships. The inventiveness of Glaswegians made them leaders in industrial processing: J. B. Neilson, who invented the hot-blast furnace, made it possible to exploit the resources of iron ore on which part of the city itself was built.

On the two separate evenings that Mendelssohn and Klingemann spent in Glasgow they possibly saw little of the city's social life, but many visitors to the city at the time commented on the large numbers of people they saw congregating on the streets. Sometimes, instead of standing at the street corners, they would take a stroll, although this was mainly the pastime of the middle classes who had their traditional walks in Great Western Road and in Sauchiehall Street. For the working classes, however, a favourite alternative was a night out in one of Glasgow's one thousand eight hundred public houses, and pay-day meant a night of oblivion to the squalor of home life and to the fatigue of long days on the factory floor. It was drink which led to most of the crime in Glasgow; arrests for being drunk and disorderly accounted for four-fifths of all prosecutions in the city's courts. In an attempt to combat the ravages of alcohol the Temperance movement was established, and since its formation coincided with the time of Mendelssohn's visit it would have been a popular topic for comment.

A Visit to Loch Lomond

On Tuesday, August 11, the two travellers set out for Loch Lomond.

Loch Lomond: August 12, 1829

Mendelssohn: Loch Lomond

Ben Lomond: August 12, 1829

Mendelssohn: The Trossachs (August 13, 1829)

Although their letters make no mention of it, it is evident from Mendelssohn's sketches that they visited the Trossachs on Thursday, August 13.

On the evening of Thursday, August 13, the travellers experienced a storm on Loch Lomond which Mendelssohn describes in a letter written later from Glasgow:

90

Glasgow: August 15, 1829

The day before yesterday on Loch Lomond we were sitting in deep twilight in a small rowing boat, and were going to cross to the opposite shore, invited by a gleaming light, when there came a sudden tremendous gust of wind from the mountain; the boat began to see-saw so fearfully that I caught up my cloak and got ready to swim. All our things were thrown topsy-turvy, and Klingemann anxiously called to me, 'Look sharp, look sharp!' But with our usual good luck we got safely through. When on shore, we had to sit in a room with a cursing young Englishman, who was something between a sportsman, a peasant, and a gentleman, perfectly insufferable, and with three other individuals of a similar kind, and were obliged to sleep in the next house close under the roof, so that from sitting-room to bedroom we walked with umbrellas, cloak, and cap.
[FMB]

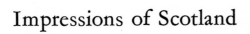

Impressions of Scotland

Ever-memorable country! The mnemonic powers of the nose are well known, and in the same ways as Walt [from Jean Paul's Flegejahre] *could not forget auriculas, so the Highland smell will be remembered by us, a certain smoky atmosphere which every Highlander has about him. I once, while going along, closed my eyes and then correctly stated that five Highlanders had passed — my nose had seen them. It is easy to determine the number of houses in the same way. As for the rest, the country is not as bad as certain people in great capitals would make out. It is almost exclusively a mountainous country, and as such it is remarkable. At night, when the storm rises, you find an inn with beds and rooms which you are not exactly obliged to share with cattle drovers, but with sporting John Bulls; if a fowl chances to run about the room or a pig squeaks under you, it is proof that you may look forward to a new-laid egg and some pork next morning at breakfast; if the cart on which you travel jolts rather murderously, that is only the more temptation to get out and walk; if no officious fellow happens to be found to carry one's things on foot, that is but a friendly invitation to make oneself comfortable and drive; if nothing is to be had but fresh herrings and beautiful rich cream, that indicates the patriarchal primitiveness which the modern world has so often on its lips; if the people make a clumsy effort at something better, with diluted wine and diluted bills, that shows a pleasing disposition for culture. Altogether the inns, so few and far between, which on the map are marked as towns, perhaps represent nothing further than seeds of cities, here and there dotted over the broad moor which by-and-by will swell and grow.*

At last we issued from the Highlands, longing for the warm sun, which we had not seen for days, lounging in good carriages long unknown to us, driving through level country and cheerful villages, such as we had not been in for ages. The sun did really shine out here from the blue sky, only over the Highlands black clouds were hanging; but the longer and oftener we looked back, the bluer and more misty grew the mountains, at the feet of which we had been lying, all deep shades of colour mingled, and we might have become Highland-sick and wished ourselves back had we now known that the reality within that mountain land was gray, cold and majestic. It was a sweet farewell to the heights which we at once abuse and love.

[CK]

To describe the wretchedness and the comfortless, inhospitable solitude of the country, time and space do not allow; we wandered ten days without meeting a single traveller; what are marked on the map as towns, or at least villages, are a few sheds, huddled together, with one hole for door, window and chimney, for the entrance and exit of men, beasts, light, and smoke, in which to all questions you get a dry 'No', in which brandy is the only beverage known, without church, without street, without gardens, the rooms pitch dark in broad daylight, children and fowls lying in the same straw, many huts without roofs, many unfinished, with crumbling walls, many ruins of burnt houses; and even these inhabited spots are but sparingly scattered over the country. Long before you arrive at a place you hear it talked of;

the rest is heath, with red or brown heather, withered fir stumps, and white stones, or black moors where they shoot grouse. Now and then you find beautiful parks, but deserted, and broad lakes, but without boats, the roads a solitude. Fancy in all that the rich glowing sunshine, which paints the heath in a thousand divinely warm colours, and then the clouds chasing hither and thither! It is no wonder that the Highlands have been called melancholy.

[FMB]

The Journey South

Glasgow: August 15, 1829

This then is the end of our Highland journey and the last of our joint letters. We have been happy together, have led a merry life, and roved about the country as gaily as if the storm and rain, of which all newspapers (by this time perhaps even the Berlin ones) are full, had not existed.
[FBM]

But two fellows have wandered merrily about them, laughed at every opportunity, rhymed and sketched together, growled at one another and at the world when they happened to be vexed or did not find anything to eat, devoured everything eatable when they did find it, and slept twelve hours every night; those two were we, who will not forget it as long as we live.
[FBM]

And now, packing and reckoning, end our four weeks' wet but good holiday. May the bells go on ringing and pealing until wayward fate again takes a fancy to separate people God knows how, and unite them God knows where.
[CK]

Mendelssohn and Klingemann left Glasgow by coach on Saturday, August 15, and the two travellers parted company at Liverpool, Klingemann returning directly to London and Mendelssohn heading off to Wales to stay with some friends.

97

The 'Scottish' Symphony of 1842

Between 1829 and his death in 1847 Mendelssohn visited England ten times, but never set foot again in Scotland following his Highland Journey. Although the inspiration for the opening of the first movement of his 'Scottish' Symphony occurred to him in 1829, it was not until 1842 that the symphony was completed and received its first performance in March of that year. He conducted at the Lower Rhine Festival at Dusseldorf in May, and shortly after, with his wife Cécile, went to England where the warm reception which he received from the Philharmonic Society on the occasion of the performance of his first symphony was repeated when, as guest of the Society, he conducted the 'Scottish' Symphony. This was a great success, and a later concert in the same Philharmonic season included the 'Hebrides' Overture.

> *Yesterday evening I played my concerto in D minor and directed my 'Hebrides' in the Philharmonic where I was received like an old friend and where they played with a degree of enthusiasm which gave me more pleasure than I can say. The people make such a fuss over me this time that I am quite dumbfounded; I believe they clapped their hands and stamped for at least ten minutes after the concerto, and insisted on the 'Hebrides' being repeated.*
> [FMB]

Socially the climax of his stay in England was the visit to Buckingham Palace where he met Queen Victoria, only twenty-three years old at the time, and Prince Albert whom she had married two years previously.

> *The details of my last visit to Buckingham Palace I must write you at once because they will amuse you so much, and me, too. As Grahl says – and it is true – the only friendly English house, one that is really comfortable and where one feels at ease, is Buckingham Palace – as a matter of fact, I know several others, but on the whole, I agree with him. Joking apart, Prince Albert had asked me to go to him on Saturday at two o'clock, so that I might try his organ before I left England. I found him all alone; and as we were talking away, the Queen came in, also alone, in a house dress. She said she was obliged to leave for Claremont in an hour; 'But,*

99

goodness! how it looks here', *she added, when she saw that the wind had littered the whole room, and even the pedals of the organ (which, by the way, made a very pretty feature in the room), with leaves of music from a large portfolio that lay open. As she spoke, she knelt down and began picking up the music; Prince Albert helped, and I too was not idle. Then Prince Albert proceeded to explain the stops to me, and while he was doing it, she said that she would put things straight alone.*

But I begged that the Prince would first play me something, so that, as I said, I might boast about it in Germany; and thereupon he played me a chorale by heart, with pedals, so charmingly and clearly and correctly that many an organist could have learned something;

. . . and the Queen, having finished her work, sat beside him and listened, very pleased. Then I had to play, and I began my chorus from 'St Paul': 'How lovely are the Messengers!' Before I got to the end of the first verse, they both began to sing the chorus very well, and all the time Prince Albert managed the stops for me so expertly – first a flute, then full at the forte, *the whole register at the D major part, then he made such an excellent* diminuendo *with the stops, and so on to the end of the piece, and all by heart – that I was heartily pleased. Then the Crown Prince of Gotha came in, and there was more conversation, and among other things the Queen asked if I had composed any new songs, and said that she was very fond of singing the published ones. 'You should sing one to him', said Prince Albert; and after a little begging she said she would try the 'Fruehlingslied' in B-flat. 'Yes, if it were still here, for all my music is packed up for Claremont.' Prince Albert went to look for it, but came back saying it was already packed. 'Oh, perhaps it could be unpacked', said I. 'We must send for Lady N. N.', said she. (I did not catch the name.) So the bell was rung, and the servants were sent after it, but came back embarrassed; and then the Queen went herself, and whilst she was gone Prince Albert said to me: 'She begs you will accept this present as a remembrance' – and gave me a case with a beautiful ring, on which is engraved 'V.R., 1842'.*

Then the Queen came back and said: 'Lady N. N. has left and has taken all my things with her. It really is most unseemly.' (You can't think how that amused me.) I then begged that I might not be made to suffer for the accident, and hoped she would sing another song. After some consultation with her husband he said: 'She will sing you something of Gluck's'. Meantime the Prince of Gotha had come in, and we five proceeded through the corridors and rooms to the Queen's sitting-room, where, next to the piano, stood an enormous, thick rocking-horse, and two great bird-cages

Queen Victoria and Prince Albert (at the organ) with Mendelssohn

*and pictures on the walls and beautifully bound books lay on the tables,
and music on the piano. The Duchess of Kent came in, too, and while
they were all talking I rummaged about a little amongst the music and found
my first set of songs. So, naturally I begged her to choose one of those rather
than the Gluck, to which she very kindly consented; and which did she
choose? 'Schöner und schöner'; sang it beautifully in tune, in strict time,
and with very nice expression. Only where, following 'Der Prosa Last und
Mueh', where it goes down to D and then comes up again by semitones, she
sang D-sharp each time; and because the first two times I gave her the note,
the last time, sure enough, she sang D – where it ought to have been D-sharp.
But except for this little mistake it was really charming, and the last long
G I have never heard better or purer or more natural from any amateur.
Then I was obliged to confess that Fanny had written the song (which I
found very hard, but pride must have a fall), and to beg her to sing one of*

*my own, too. 'If I would give her plenty of help she would gladly try', she
said, and sang 'Lass dich nur nichts dauern' really without a mistake, and
with charming feeling and expression. I thought to myself that one must not
pay too many compliments on such an occasion, so I merely thanked her very
much; but she said, 'Oh, if only I had not been so nervous; otherwise I really
have a long breath'. Then I praised her heartily, and with the best
conscience in the world; for just that part with the long C at the close she
had done so well, taking it and the three notes next to it all in the same
breath, as one seldom hears it done, and therefore it amused me doubly that
she herself should have begun about it.*

*After this Prince Albert sang the Erntelied, 'Es ist ein Schnitter', and then
he said I must play him something before I went, and gave me as themes the
chorale which he had played on the organ and the song he had just sung.
If everything had gone as usual, I ought to have improvised dreadfully
badly; for that is what nearly always happens to me when I want to it go
well, and then I should have gone away vexed with the whole morning. But
just as if I were to keep the nicest, most charming recollection of it,
without any unpleasantness at all, I have rarely improvised as well. I was in
the mood for it, and played a long time, and enjoyed it myself; of course,
besides the two themes, I also brought in the songs the Queen had sung; but
it all worked in so naturally that I would have been glad not to stop. And
they followed me with so much intelligence and attention that I felt more at
my ease than I ever have in improvising before an audience. Well, and then
she said, 'I hope you will come and visit us soon again in England', and
then I took my leave; and down below I saw the beautiful carriages waiting,
with their scarlet outriders, and in a quarter of an hour the flag was lowered,
and the papers said: 'Her Majesty left the Palace at 30 minutes past 3'.
I walked back through the rain to Klingemann's, and enjoyed more than
everything giving a piping-hot account of it all to him and Cécile. It was
a delightful morning! I must add that I asked permission to dedicate my A
minor symphony to the Queen, that having really been the reason for my
visit to England, and because the English name would be doubly suited to the
Scottish piece; and that, just as the Queen was going to sing, she said: 'But
the parrot must be removed first, or he will scream louder than I sing'; upon
which Prince Albert rang the bell and the Prince of Gotha said: 'I will carry
him out,' upon which I replied, 'Allow me to do that', (like cousin Wolf
with his 'allow me, me, me!') and lifted up the big cage and carried it out to
the astonished servants, etc. There is much more to tell when we meet, but if
this long description makes Dirichlet set me down as an aristocrat, tell him
that I swear that I am a greater radical than ever.*

The entries at this time in Queen Victoria's *Journal* view the meetings with Mendelssohn in similar enthusiastic terms.

Buckingham Palace

June 16, 1842. . . After dinner came Mendelssohn Bartholdy, whose acquaintance I was so anxious to make. Albert had already seen him the other morning. He is short, dark, and Jewish looking – delicate – with a fine intellectual forehead. I should say he must be about 35 or 6. He is very pleasing and modest, and is greatly protected by the King of Prussia. He played first of all some of his 'Lieder ohne Worte' after which, his Serenade and then, he asked us to give him a theme, upon which he could improvise. We gave him two, 'Rule Britannia', and the Austrian National Anthem. He began immediately, and really I have never heard anything so beautiful; the way in which he blended them both together and changed over from one to the other, was quite wonderful as well as the exquisite harmony and feelings he puts into the variations, and the powerful rich chords, and modulations, which reminded one of all his beautiful compositions. At one moment he played the Austrian Anthem with the right hand while he played 'Rule Britannia', as the bass, with his left! He made some further improvisations on well known themes and songs. We were all filled with the greatest admiration. Poor Mendelssohn was quite exhausted, when he had done playing.

Claremont

July 9. . . Mendelssohn came to take leave of Albert, previous to his returning to Germany, and he was good enough to play for us, on Albert's organ, which he did beautifully. As he wished to hear me sing, we took him over to our large room, where, with some trepidation, I sang, accompanied by him, first, a song which I thought was his composition, but which he said was his sister's, and then one of his beautiful ones, after which he played to us a little. We thanked him very much, and I gave him a handsome ring as a remembrance.

Much has already been written about various aspects of the 'Scottish' Symphony, so what remains to be said is perhaps best framed as a commentary on the commentaries of others. Authorities have remarked on the pictorial nature of Mendelssohn's music, reading, for example, into the slow movement of the symphony a 'warrior's lament' and into the finale a 'wild highland fling', a 'gathering of clan chiefs', the 'savage interplay of claymore and dirk'. How far it is wise to attribute to the composer the presence of such ideas in his mind is a matter for speculation and not dogmatic foisting of interpretations on the music.

We must take Mendelssohn's word for the fact that the musical ideas of the slow introduction to the first movement occurred to him in the Palace of Holyrood on his visit to Edinburgh, and we can reasonably comment on his use of classical symphonic forms in as far as they deviate from the norm, if there is such a thing, but this is as far as we should go. A storm episode towards the end of this movement was in character with the weather he experienced in Scotland, but musically it follows similar storm episodes in the music of both Beethoven ('Pastoral' Symphony, 1809) and Rossini ('William Tell' Overture, composed in a significant year from our point of view: 1829), and anticipates by eight years a highly derivative passage in Liszt's *Les Préludes*.

Almost all commentators on the work refer to the linking of the first movement to the scherzo, and suggest that this was perhaps due to Mendelssohn's dislike of applause between the movements of a piece – he was annoyed when the Philharmonic audience demanded an encore of the scherzo in his First Symphony. The actual link of the first movement to the scherzo achieved by a few quiet, detached chords, followed by a pause, is not greatly inspired (unlike that between the first and second movements of his Violin Concerto), and indeed there is an actual break of silence between the two movements, but surely the point is that the music carries through as long as the conductor has his arm poised to continue. It is in this sense that the link between the first two movements is not a positive one but a negative one; the music of the first movement is not brought to a conclusion in the traditional manner of symphonic first movements.

The second movement introduces a tune which is based on the five notes of the pentatonic scale characteristic of Scots' (amongst other nations') folk-music, but the tune has neither the shape nor the monotony of most traditional melodies. The rhythm with which the tune ends has been compared to the rhythmic 'snap' which is also a feature of Scots' folk-music, but again this comparison is imprecise since the Scotch snap has a sharper, more precise rhythmic character than that used by Mendelssohn.

The borderline between genuine emotion and sentimentality is an indistinct one, and one which Mendelssohn's music forces us to consider. The style of the slow movement is such that it is possible to distort the emotional content of the music so that it crosses the border into sentimentality; the sensitive performance will show an awareness of this problem and will take care not to lay undue emphasis on melodic phrasing or over-dramatising harmonic discords and resolutions. Mendelssohn has also been criticised for the 'moralising' of the tail-piece to his finale, but such an interpretation says more about the prejudices of commentators reacting against Victorian attitudes than it does about the fact that Mendelssohn's music simply lacks sufficient interest at this point of climax: to play the same tune three times, only louder, is just not good enough.

The intensity of Mendelssohn's feeling for Britain is revealed both in his letters and by the frequency of his visits, and is endorsed by the composition of certain works. Mendelssohn's feelings of affection towards Britain were reciprocated, as we have seen, from Queen Victoria and Prince Albert downwards, but the reason for the relationship of two such unlike partners – a Berlin Jew and a race of John Bulls, to use Klingemann's words – is something of an enigma. Englishmen found in Mendelssohn just that combination of qualities which they respected most: conservatism, unfailing good manners, and an easy personality in company. Mendelssohn found in the English positive qualities of friendship and appreciation and a warmth of welcome in Britain which he lacked in Berlin and to which he failed to respond in Paris.

> *I should like now to play my* Calm Sea *etc. for the public here, and they would grasp and understand it much better than the circle of cultivated people in our salon. And yet they understand nothing of music . . . Also, by God, I play better here than in Berlin, and just because the people listen with more pleasure.*
> [FMB]

The musical life of Italy, dominated as it was by opera, had little to offer Mendelssohn whose preference was to compose instrumental and orchestral music. The great days of the First Viennese School were over, and triviality replaced the great symphonic style of Mozart, Beethoven and Schubert. There was something about the French attitude to music which Mendelssohn disliked; besides charlatanry, which produced music of supreme inconsequence, he disapproved of the open exhibition of eroticism shown on stage in such operas as *Robert le Diable*.

> *It made a sensation, but I would not like to have that sort of thing in any opera of mine for it is vulgar, and if that is the sort of thing that spells success these days, I prefer to write church music.*
> [FMB]

Mendelssohn's visits to Britain highlight the changing role and status of the musician in the early nineteenth century. Unlike his idol, J. S. Bach, who probably thought of himself as a master-craftsman providing a service for which there was a demand in the courts and churches of Germany in the second half of the seventeenth century, musicians after the end of the eighteenth century stopped thinking of themselves in this way. The Romantic musician was viewed by himself and society as a creative artist, and the possessor of a rare talent. Good musicians were regarded highly in society, and, given the great ability and temperament of a Mendelssohn, the artist was looked upon as a genius. This change in status and how it occurred is of particular interest in the case of Mendelssohn, remembering his special affinity to the music of the past. During the eighteenth century the erosion of many of the traditional barriers in the German class structure had taken place and it was possible to move from a position of poverty to one of wealth and considerable social influence. The fortunes of the Mendelssohn family changed in this way and demonstrated that the movement of individuals from the lower social classes into the growing middle classes of people in commerce and the professions was possible. Having achieved this new social standing the musician became a new kind of professional, supported financially in a different way. It was only when the middle classes gradually began taking over patronage of the arts from the aristocracy that this change became possible. J. S. Bach experienced the patronage of both the church and court, and when society at large took over the role of these institutions with respect to the arts this marked the end of the system of employment of musicians which had been in operation for over two hundred years.

The assertiveness of the middle class in the revolutionary closing years of the eighteenth century is shown in their dissatisfaction with the results of traditional musical patronage, and this allowed the musician a new freedom to work how and where he pleased. Mendelssohn enjoyed the support of the middle-class paying public which built large concert halls and accepted concert-going as a natural feature of the cultured scene.

The change in the status of the musician is nowhere more clearly defined than in the relationship between Mendelssohn and Queen Victoria and her Consort by whom he was treated with warm respect. As accomplished musical amateurs the royal couple responded with admiration to the superb professionalism of Mendelssohn, and it was perhaps the fact that they themselves learned and performed music that produced such a pleasurable and easy relationship. Their friendship was extended to Mendelssohn's widow after the composer's early death at the age of thirty-eight, and her reply to the Queen's expression of sympathy suggests a level of communication between a

Title page of 'Scotch' Symphony (1843) indicating Mendelssohn's dedication of his composition to Queen Victoria of England

musician's family and royalty which would have been unthinkable even a few decades previously:

> *Your Majesty has graciously expressed her keen sympathy in the tragic loss which has just been inflicted upon me. If anything could console me for the cruel sorrow which I have just experienced, it would be the affection shown to me from all quarters, and by Your Majesty and His Royal Highness, Prince Albert.*
>
> *Unhappily, in such a trial, there is no human consolation. Thanks to the infinite mercy of God, I shall follow alone a path bare of all joy.*
>
> *In expressing to Your Majesty and to His Royal Highness, Prince Albert, my profoundest gratitude for his kind sympathy,*
>
> > *I remain, your very humble,*
> > *Cécile Mendelssohn Bartholdy.*

Appendix: Summary of the Highland Journey of 1829

Saturday, August 1	Departure from Edinburgh
Sunday, August 2	Sketching near Dunkeld
Monday, August 3	To Blair Athol before proceeding to Bridge of Tummel
Tuesday, August 4	Visit to Falls of Moness
Wednesday, August 5	Sketching near Loch Tay and Ben More
Thursday, August 6	Trip by cart to Fort William
Friday, August 7	Journey via Oban to Tobermory
Saturday, August 8	5 am put to sea: visit Staffa and Iona
	7 pm arrive Tobermory
Sunday, August 9	6.30 am arrive Oban and proceed to Inveraray
Monday, August 10	Set out from Inveraray in a steam-boat then travel short distance by land to Loch Eck, board steamer and change steamer at the mouth of Clyde.
	Sail up Clyde to Glasgow, past Dumbarton Castle and Ben Lomond
Tuesday, August 11	Visit to Loch Lomond
Wednesday, August 12	
Thursday, August 13	Visit to Trossachs and storm episode on Loch Lomond
Friday, August 14	Return to Glasgow
Saturday, August 15	Leave Glasgow to travel to Cumberland

A Select Bibliography

Grove, Sir George, *Dictionary of Music and Musicians*, Volume 3, ed. H. C. Colles (Macmillan, 1928)

Haldane, A. R. B., *Three Centuries of Scottish Posts* (Edinburgh Univeristy Press, 1971)

Hendrie, Gerald, *Mendelssohn's Rediscovery of Bach* (Humanities: A Foundation Course, Units 27–8) (Open Univeristy Press, 1971)

Kellett, John R., *Glasgow* (Blond, 1967)

Lockspeiser, Edward, *Music and Painting* (Cassell, 1973)

Maxwell-Scott, Sir Walter, *Abbotsford*, rev. ed. James Corson (Abbotsford, 1975)

Richards, John, *Stagecoach* (BBC, 1976)

Scharf, Aaron, *Romanticism* (Arts: A Second Level Course 'The Age of Revolutions', Units 33–4) (Open University Press, 1972)

Youngson, A. J., *The Making of Classical Edinburgh* (Edinburgh University Press, 1966)

Acknowledgements

The Mendelssohn Family from Letters & Journal, Vol. 1
Sebastian Hensel (trans. Carl Klingemann and an American collaborator) by kind permission of PURNELL BOOKS, originally published by Sampson Low, Marston, Searle and Rivington in London 1881.

Felix Mendelssohn: Letters
edited by G. Selden Goth by kind permission of VIENNA HOUSE, New York.

Mendelssohn: Letters & Recollections
by Dr. Ferdinand Hiller (trans. M. E. von Glehn) by kind permission of MACMILLAN BOOKS LONDON & BASINGSTOKE, originally published by MacMillan & Co. 1874.

My Recollections of Felix Mendelssohn Bartholdy and his Letters to Me
by Philipp Eduard Devrient (trans. Natalia Macfarren) by kind permission of MACMILLAN LONDON & BASINGSTOKE, originally published by Richard Bentley, 1869.

Entries from *Queen Victoria's Journal*
by the gracious permission of HER MAJESTY THE QUEEN.

ACKNOWLEDGEMENTS

The authors and publisher would like to gratefully acknowledge the sources mentioned below for their kindness and co-operation in allowing the use of their illustrations throughout this book.

Bildarchiv Preussischer Kulturbesitz

J. W. Childe's watercolour portrait of Mendelssohn (1829)
Moses Mendelssohn (1729–1788), grandfather of Felix
Abraham Mendelssohn (1776–1835), father of Felix
Lea Mendelssohn, née Salomon (1777–1842) mother of Felix
Fanny Cäcilie, Felix Mendelssohn's elder sister
Rebecka, his younger sister
Paul, his younger brother
The Mendelssohn's house and garden in Berlin

Bodleian Library

Mendelssohn: sketch of York (July 23, 1829)
Mendelssohn: Durham Cathedral from the west (July 24, 1829)
Mendelssohn: Edinburgh skyline from Arthur's Seat
Mendelssohn: Birnam Wood near Dunkeld
Mendelssohn: The Rumbling Bridge near Dunkeld
Mendelssohn: Falls of Moness, Birks of Aberfeldy
Mendelssohn: Falls of Moness, Birks of Aberfeldy
Mendelssohn: the foot of Ben More
Mendelssohn: view towards the Hebrides
Mendelssohn: Loch Lomond
Mendelssohn: The Trossachs (August 13, 1829)
Title page of 'Scotch' Symphony (1843) indicating Mendelssohn's dedication of
*   his composition to Queen Victoria of England*

Mansell Collection

Queen Victoria and Prince Albert (at the organ) with Mendelssohn
Castle & Grassmarket, Edinburgh
Sir Walter Scott, from the original by J. P. Knight
Dumbarton Castle from the Clyde
The Old Tower near Lanark (1828) by R. P. Bonington
Mendelssohn
Aubrey Beardsley's portrait of Mendelssohn, from 'The Savoy' magazine 1896
Coach outside the Bull & Mouth, St. Martins-le-Grand, by Shayer
Johann Wolfgang von Goethe (1749–1832)

115

Mrs. R. B. Gotch
  Carl Klingemann – taken from Mendelssohn and his friends in Kensington
  by R. B. Gotch

Le Directeur de Musee du Louvre
  Apollo Slaying Python (1849) by Delacroix

Edinburgh City Library
  Edinburgh from the west end of Princes Street, 1824
  Map of Edinburgh

Barnaby's Picture Library
  Fingal's Cave from the sea

Lord Astor of Hever (private collection)
  J. M. W. Turner: Staffa, Fingal's Cave (1832)

Royal Academy of Arts
  John Flaxman: Ulysses Slaying the Suitors (1793)

Mitchell Library Glasgow
  Joseph Swan: The Broomielaw (circa 1825)

Graphische Sammlung Albertina
  Hamburg Port in the eighteenth century

Madame J. L. Vaudoyer
  Delacroix: La Malibran